W9-BNH-366

ESSENCE OF CHRISTIANITY

ESSENCE OF CHRISTIANITY

Two Essays

By
ANDERS NYGREN

Translated by
PHILIP S. WATSON

WITHDRAWN

Theodore Lownik Library
Illinois Benedictine College
Lisle, Illinois 60532

LONDON
THE EPWORTH PRESS

FIRST PUBLISHED IN 1960

© THE EPWORTH PRESS 1960

201
N994e

PRINTED AND BOUND IN ENGLAND BY
HAZELL WATSON AND VINEY LTD
AYLESBURY AND SLOUGH

CONTENTS

CONTENTS

TRANSLATOR'S NOTE

THE TWO ESSAYS contained in this volume were originally published in Swedish in 1922 and 1932 under the titles of *Det bestående i kristendomen* and *Försoningen en Guds-gärning* respectively. The first of them has been much used in Sweden as an introductory text-book for theological students. It outlines in non-technical and more or less popular form the philosophy of religion underlying its author's theological work. Since none of his quite substantial philosophical writings is available in English, this essay can well serve as an introduction to his thought in that field for English readers. It furnishes something of the background against which *Agape and Eros,* for example, was written and can most profitably be read. It is also not irrelevant, despite the lapse of time since its original publication, to contemporary discussions of the meaning of religious language and ideas.

The second essay elaborates a theme which in the first is claimed as a quite central concern of all religion and not least of Christianity. It also illustrates something of the theological implications of the idea of Agape, which is basic to the whole of Anders Nygren's theology. The rendering of the word *försoningen,* in the title and elsewhere, has caused some difficulty, since it is the equivalent of both 'atonement' and 'reconciliation'. In most cases the former has been the obvious choice, in a few the latter; but sometimes it has seemed desirable to use both words, particularly in contexts where there is a reference to 2 Corinthians 5^{18-19}, the text which is so central to the whole argument of the essay.

PHILIP S. WATSON

7

THE PERMANENT ELEMENT
IN CHRISTIANITY

ONE

Introductory

IT IS NOW well over a hundred and fifty years since Voltaire made his famous pronouncement that it would not be more than a hundred years before Christianity had vanished from the earth. This was neither the first nor the last time that Christianity has had its death certificate written out in advance by its opponents. But in spite of all such prophecies, Christianity persists in surviving as a force in the life both of individuals and society. No one knowing the facts could very well assert that Christianity, either in intensity or in capacity for expansion, exhibits now a vitality less than in Voltaire's day.

Christianity persists. But that is by no means to say that it persists entirely unchanged throughout the ages. To many people, it is true, the idea that with the passage of time Christianity has undergone all kinds of changes, is strange and uncongenial. They would like to regard Christianity as something absolutely unchanging, of which not 'one jot or one tittle' can be altered. The reason for this is easy to understand. They are convinced of the eternal significance of Christianity, and think they can maintain it only by ascribing to it the unchanging character of the eternal. These two ideas, however, have nothing to do with one another. We may even find it easier to preserve our conviction of the eternal significance of Christianity when we see how it appears at different times in quite different guises, than we could if it were static and immutable. No one need refuse, because he is convinced of the imperishable worth of Christianity, to acknowledge the obvious fact that it is continually developing and undergoing change.

That Christianity is not immutable is plain from the fact that it has a history. Anything that is immutable has no history, or at all events a most uninteresting one. Thus the traditional conception of the Reformation, for example, as simply a restoration of Christianity in its original form, clearly shows a very imperfect understanding of what the Reformation means. A truer picture is given only when emphasis is laid rather on the renewal of Christianity than on its restoration—an idea with which Luther himself was not unfamiliar. For although Luther often thinks of his work as a restoration of the original Christian message and a return to the Pauline gospel, yet he also represents himself as one through whom God was speaking to his own day and generation, just as He spoke to Israel of old through the prophets. It was not without consequence that Paul lived and worked in the first century, in an environment of Judaism and Hellenism, whereas Luther in the sixteenth century was surrounded by the Renaissance and Catholicism in a patriarchal, bourgeois society. Christianity has discarded in Luther much of the historical dress and colouring which it possessed in primitive Christian times, and many of Luther's historically conditioned ideas have disappeared from modern evangelical Christianity.

Any simile is imperfect, but we may perhaps venture a simile to illustrate the relation of Christianity to the changes and chances of human life, and the extent to which it is influenced by different ages and cultures. We must not, however, compare it to a stone thrown into the water, which affects its environment by setting up undulations, but which itself remains unchanging and impenetrable, receiving no impressions from its environment. Christianity may rather be compared to a plant, which builds up its organism by taking into itself and assimilating materials from its environment. The plant preserves its own structure in all circumstances, and puts its own stamp on everything that is incorporated into its organism; yet at the same time, while never losing the characteristics of its species, it can assume the most varied forms according to the soil, the climate, the season, and so forth. The birch is a good example. Whether we find it in the form with which we are familiar, or as a dwarf tree in a more arctic climate, whether it is in the full green of summer, or stands lifeless and bare—everywhere it preserves its own structure. It is a birch and nothing else. Yet at the same time it bears plain marks of the climate and the season. So it is with Christianity. Wherever we come across it, it bears the marks of the age, the people, the culture, within which it lives; yet it does this without surrendering its definite Christian structure.

If then we cannot say that Christianity is in all ages an unchanging phenomenon, and yet we affirm that Christianity itself persists, it is incumbent on us to give an answer to the question, what exactly is it that persists in Christianity? What is that structure of Christianity which persists without suffering the encroachment of all those changes of time and circumstance in which Christianity meets us? In other words, we must discuss the question of the permanent element in Christianity.

As it stands, however, this question is ambiguous. We must therefore pause for a moment in order to define its meaning more precisely. And perhaps it will be best to say first what we do *not* mean by our question.

When people speak of the permanent element in Christianity, they often have a singularly superficial conception of what this means, a conception which we might describe more or less as follows. When Christianity first saw the light, nearly two thousand years ago, it comprised a number of articles of belief concerning God, the creation and constitution of the world, angels and demons, man, his creation and original state, his fall and redemption, Christ as God and man in one Person, the end of the world and

13

the last judgement, and so forth. This and much else of a similar kind is supposed to have formed the original substance of Christianity. But, the argument proceeds, the two thousand years which have gone by since then, have not passed without leaving their mark. A tireless criticism has been directed against now one now another of these points of doctrine. Natural science, history and philosophy have all contributed to the criticism. Above all, we now possess a quite different view of the world from that of two thousand years ago. Then men lived in the conviction that the earth was the centre of the universe, and they had therefore no difficulty in conceiving the whole of existence as designed to further the interests of the human race. Everything was viewed in the light of its significance for man. But now we know that our earth is merely a speck of dust in the universe, merely one among millions of worlds, to which we quite arbitrarily attribute such great importance, just because it happens to be 'our' earth. The widening of our horizon to infinity results in the shrinking of our own existence to the infinitesimal. Surely it is meaningless to suppose that just this little spot in the universe could be the stage of such a mighty drama as Christianity unfolds for us! Similarly with regard to time. Two thousand years ago it was easy to talk of the beginning and end of the world, since the existence of the world was reckoned in only a few thousand years, or at most in a number of successive ages which were relatively easy to measure. It was then not difficult to think of that bit of history with the making of which we are concerned, as an important phase in the realization of the all-embracing kingdom of God. But now, when we reckon with immeasurable vistas of time in the evolution of the world prior to all human history, and with an immeasurable future, the time occupied by the history of humanity shrinks to something infinitesimal. Is it not absurd to want to include in this period of time, as Christianity does, a history of God with humanity?—Arguments like these illustrate how cosmology can be brought into relation with Christianity, and how support can be found in natural science, history and philosophy for a criticism of Christian ideas.

The combined effect of all these circumstances, it is supposed, has necessitated the discarding of one bit of Christianity after another. Hence the very common notion has arisen, that the only Christianity an educated modern man can accept is merely a small fraction of original Christianity. And naturally we must assume that the process will continue in the same direction, so that the fraction will become less and less as time goes on. But when Christianity is again and again whittled down like this, and the original Christian capital keeps on dwindling, we can hardly help asking ourselves how far the dissolution is to go. Is there to be finally nothing left of Christianity at all? Or is there some remnant, however small, which can never be discarded? Is there any permanent element in Christianity, anything which possesses eternal validity? And if so, what is this permanent element?

When the subject is approached from this angle, it is easy to understand why people look, as they so often do nowadays, to the philosophy of religion for a solution of the religious problem. Where else should an answer be forthcoming to the question, what is of permanent value in Christianity? The chief task of philosophy is to distinguish between what is valid and what is invalid. Have we not therefore the right to expect the philosophy of religion, if it deserves its name, to distinguish between the husk and the kernel of Christianity, or between the historical trappings which can be abandoned without loss, and the elements of permanent value and eternal validity which both can and must be held fast? It might seem to be so; yet this whole method of approach is mistaken. To inquire about the permanent element in Christianity in this sense is to display no very great discernment. It would be easy to produce a whole series of reasons why the question cannot be put in this way, but here it must suffice to point out a few of the main objections.

In the first place, Christianity is not originally a certain number of ideas or beliefs. The very starting-point is false. Secondly—and this objection is connected with the first— no single part of Christianity has ever yet given way before scientific, historical, or philosophical criticism, or because of a change in cosmology.

The latter assertion may at first sight seem startling. We are so much in the habit of thinking of the Christian faith as if it were on the same level as scientific knowledge, that we are apt to assume that any advance in scientific knowledge, any change in the general picture of the world, will require a corresponding revision of Christianity—just as, on the other hand, when we observe a change in the religious situation, we are at once ready to seek its cause in a non-religious development. As against this widespread idea, we shall show in what follows that religion is an original and independent type of spiritual life, which obeys its own laws; and that being so, it is clear that Christianity can never be touched by any non-religious criticism whatsoever, whether scientific or of any other kind. Within its sphere it is completely autonomous. Just as science is amenable only to scientific criticism, and ethics only to criticism from an ethical standpoint, so religion is amenable only to religious criticism. Religion admits of no negative criticism, but only of that self-criticism which arises from the fact that religion outgrows itself. If, for example, under the influence of Western civilization, the fetish-worshipper allows himself to be drawn away from fetishism, this does not mean, as is commonly assumed, that he advances to a higher religious level. On the contrary, it may in many cases involve religious degeneration. We can only speak of religious progress if the fetish-worshipper abandons his fetishism because he perceives its *religious* deficiency, since it can no longer satisfy his religious needs—in a word, because he has grown religiously out of his earlier religious position and now feels it to be irreligious.

Only the naïve or thoughtless can ally themselves with the view that Christianity has gradually suffered the loss of one bit of its original territory after another as a result of criticism directed against it from without. Only the naïve or thoughtless can ask in this sense what is the permanent element in Christianity; that is, what little remnant is still able to survive unembarrassed by criticism.

Nor can this way of looking at things pride itself on being particularly modern or pertinent. Historically it belongs, not to our time, but to the age of the Enlightenment a hundred and fifty or more years ago, when the attempt was made to rescue a rational and tenable kernel out of Christianity, which went under the name of 'rational religion'. No doubt injustice has often been done to the honest old rationalists, inasmuch as it has become fashionable to regard them simply with pitying contempt. They cannot fairly be thought to have meant any harm to Christianity, just as they cannot be held accountable for the rather shallow treatment which 'reason' received at their hands. Yet in justice to the facts, we cannot acquit them of the charge that the result of all their endeavours to demonstrate and prove their 'rational religion' was simply the plainest demonstration and proof that they understood neither reason nor religion, neither Christianity nor philosophy.

Even so, we have no guarantee that this attitude of mind, long out of date though it essentially is, cannot conceal itself in modern treatments of the subject. It is significant, for instance, that a study in the philosophy of religion such as *Der Wahrheitsgehalt der Religion* by Rudolf Eucken concludes with an analysis which specifically aims at separating what is eternal in Christianity from what is temporal. We know in advance that all such attempts are bound to fail, yet they make their appearance with a persistence that defies refutation. Why should this be so? In point of fact, it is due to a very ancient and apparently ineradicable illusion. We have referred above to the significance of the fact that Christianity has a history; that is to say, it does not remain a constant and unchanging phenomenon throughout the ages, but is continually developing and growing. This is plain from the very different aspects which it presents at different times and in different circumstances. What appears to one age to be the most important and essential thing in Christianity, will be thrust into the background by a succeeding generation, and in its place other aspects will be brought forward and regarded as of the essence of the matter. All this is entirely justifiable. Against such a change in emphasis, which occurs as it were automatically and without conscious intent, no legitimate objection can be brought, for it arises out of the very nature of the case. Every age has the right to see and solve its problems in its own light. But then the illusion, the ineradicable illusion, enters in. Every age is apt to assert as the permanent and eternal element in Christianity just that which is of chief interest and importance for itself. Those aspects which have previously been thought to be most essential, are from this point of view naturally judged to be unimportant accessories. The permanent element in Christianity is taken to be that of which the meaning and importance are understood and valued at the moment. The present always feels itself to be in the right as opposed to the past, and this feeling finds particularly strong expression when what is recognized as valid in the present is elevated to permanent and eternal validity. It is, of course, an unfortunate fact that the present is followed and displaced by the future, and so forfeits its claim to be right; but this is apt to be overlooked. How often the thing proclaimed in one age as the permanent and eternal element in Christianity has proved in a subsequent age to be a form of Christianity in the highest degree historically conditioned! We have seen this happen time after time. Ought we not to have learnt from it that even we ourselves are in this respect no exception to the rule? We too are situated entirely within the context of history. What counts as the present for us is not the eternal present, but something which tomorrow will be past. We ought, then, to have outgrown the illusion that we can distinguish and separate what is eternally valid from the historical form of Christianity. Let us call things by their proper names. What we do is simply to clothe Christianity in a new historical garb.

To anyone who has really thought this out, the question of the permanent element in Christianity can no longer be of any interest when it implies the attempt to extract an abiding kernel out of the transient historical husk. If the permanent element in Christianity is to be spoken of in that kind of way at all, we must have in mind, not one or another aspect of Christianity, but rather the amazing vitality whereby Christianity is enabled in every new age and situation to present an aspect which supplies just what the new conditions demand. From this point of view, the permanent element in Christianity will be its dynamic character, its unceasing capacity for creating new historical forms, whereby it makes contact with life as it is lived at every point.

Having criticized the attempt to discover the permanent element in Christianity by getting rid of everything historical and simply retaining what is eternally valid, we must now show more precisely in what sense we can and ought to raise the question of the permanent element in Christianity. We have found that Christianity is a spiritual force which perpetually creates new forms for itself. There is no simple, standard type which we can put forward with the claim that this and nothing else is Christianity. On the contrary, Christianity presents itself to us in an endless multiplicity of forms. Anyone with a little knowledge of its history is aware, for example, that Christianity did not mean the same thing to Origen as to the Apologists, to Luther as to Augustine, to Francis as to Thomas Aquinas. The manifold variety that exists is too plain to need further illustration. Forms of worship, doctrinal views, and ideals of life vary at different times and in different parts of Christendom. Is there anything permanent amid all this change? The situation looks almost hopeless. Yet we are convinced that there is something abiding here. When we give to all these different forms the common name of Christianity, we take it for granted that there is, in spite of their differences, something common to them all. We discover also that our question has now acquired an entirely different meaning. With this host of different forms of Christianity before us, we still ask what is the permanent element in Christianity. But it is no longer a question of how far there exists some little remnant of Christianity, some rationally unobjectionable trifle, which can pass without comment into the consciousness of an educated modern man and take its place among his spiritual effects. The question is rather, what is it that is specifically Christian in all these different forms, what is it that must be found in each and all of them if they have any right to bear the name of Christianity? We may therefore now restate the question of the permanent element in Christianity thus: What is it that makes Christianity what it is? What is it that must in no circumstances be lacking if we are to speak of Christianity at all? What is the specifically Christian thing in Christianity? In a word, the question concerns the essence of Christianity.

The usual practice when the essence of Christianity is under discussion, is to conceive this as an historical problem. Then, in contrast to the degeneracy of later Christianity, the essence of Christianity is found in its original, pure form, the teaching and preaching of Jesus himself. But this gives rise to several difficulties. There are things undoubt-

edly found in the message of Jesus, which we are nevertheless not disposed to recognize as belonging to the essence
of Christianity. Part of the message of Jesus, for instance,
was undeniably the thought of the speedy end of the
present age. Indeed, recent historical and critical research
has made it probable that this thought occupied a far more
central place and was far more essential than was hitherto
supposed. And that would be decisive if the question of the
essence of Christianity were a purely historical problem.
But when there is reluctance to admit that the apocalyptic-
eschatological outlook is constitutive of Christianity, it is
clear that something quite different from historical considerations is really decisive here. Our refusal to admit that
the outlook in question is of the essence of Christianity, is
obviously connected with the fact that we have no use for
it. So what we can find use for may belong to the essence
of Christianity, but the rest may not! We have evidently
returned to the very conception which we just now abandoned as unworkable.

There is much that might be said in criticism of this way
of determining the essence of Christianity, but here we will
confine ourselves to a single point: its methodological weakness. It dictates in a purely arbitrary manner what is to be
regarded as the essence of Christianity, or the permanent
element, the specifically Christian thing in Christianity. In
such circumstances it is quite natural that no agreement can
be reached, but one points to one thing, another to another,
as the permanent element in Christianity. Pure subjectivity
is the deciding factor.

If the attempt to determine the permanent element in
Christianity is to have any meaning, this arbitrariness must
cease. Mere chance or subjective inclination must not be
allowed to decide what we consider to be essential in Christianity. It cannot be too strongly insisted that we must demand the strictest objectivity in this matter. Our task in
what follows, therefore, will be to show that it is possible to

reach an objective determination of the essence of Christianity, and to indicate the means we must use to this end.

The difficulty we have to overcome is this. Owing to the multiplicity of forms in which Christianity appears, it will always seem more or less arbitrary to take any one of them as a primary basis for our determination of the essence of Christianity. But this difficulty might perhaps be avoided by starting from an entirely different point. Christianity is at all events a religion, and requires to be judged as such. If therefore we could take as our starting-point the essence of *religion*, and then show what specially characterizes Christianity as distinct from other religions, we should have found a means of establishing the characteristic and permanent element in Christianity without being obliged to set the different forms of Christianity over against one another.

If, however, we begin by asking what the permanent element in religion is (in the sense of the characteristic essence of all religion), we soon find ourselves in a difficulty exactly parallel to the one we were trying to avoid with regard to Christianity. We have no standard type of religion to which we can point and say: this and nothing else is religion. Religion meets us in an endless multiplicity of forms; and it has always proved impossible to discover by historical methods what the permanent, constant, characteristic, and essential element in all religion is. If we pick out the characteristic features chiefly from particular religions, the result will be that others are missed, and thus it will always appear more or less arbitrary which religions we select as a basis for the determination of the essence of religion. If we wish to secure a fixed starting-point, we cannot halt our quest at the religions, but must take it a stage yet farther back. That is to say, we must trace religion back to its place in the life of the spirit.

Whatever else religion may be, it is at all events a form of spiritual life. If we could start from the life of the spirit, therefore, and show what is distinctive of religion as contrasted with other kinds of spiritual life, we should have found a means of establishing what is characteristic of religion, the permanent element or essence of religion. We should thus avoid the risk of taking sides, so to speak, or of favouring certain religions at the expense of others by letting them unduly influence our definition of the essence of religion.

The lines on which our discussion must now proceed are therefore clear. We must start from *the life of the spirit* (Chapter 2), and our immediate task will be to show the necessary place of religion within it. To borrow an expression from another field, we have to find the 'geometrical locus' of religion within the life of the spirit. As the geometer looks for the centre from which he can proceed to define the circle, so we must look for the central point in the context of the spiritual life from which religion can be defined. When we have found this point, we shall be able to use it in order to draw the circumference within which religion is situated. But that will not suffice for a more precise definition of religion as regards its content. We shall have marked the boundaries of the religious terrain, but this terrain will still lie before us as an unknown land. Our next task, therefore, will be to explore and chart this *terra incognita*, so as to give a more detailed account of the specific nature of *religion* (Chapter 3). For this purpose our guide and compass will be the understanding we have gained by setting religion in its place within the life of the spirit. The contents of the picture, however, can only be obtained from empirical observation of religion as it actually exists. Only by this method can we clear the way for our third task, the examination of *Christianity* (Chapter 4), which is the main object of our inquiry. We can then discover the place of Christianity among the religions, and thus indirectly its place within the life of the spirit, the specific nature of Christianity and the permanent element

23

in Christianity. To this we may add as a fourth task a consideration of *Evangelical Christianity* (Chapter 5) and the extent to which it gives expression to the essence and specific nature of religion in general and Christianity in particular.

TWO

The Life of the Spirit

IN ATTEMPTING to establish the specific nature of Christianity we were compelled by reason of the manifold forms of Christianity to go back to religion. In attempting to establish the specific nature of religion we were forced by reason of the multiplicity we found there too, to go a stage still farther back to the life of the spirit. What is religion in the context of the life of the spirit? What aspect of the spiritual life does it represent? We have taken our question as far back as we possibly can. It is impossible in the nature of the case to go farther back to anything more fundamental. Here then we can stop. For even though the life of the spirit may quite rightly be said to include an endless multiplicity of forms, it moves nevertheless along only a few main lines. Wherever it is possible to speak of any real spiritual life, we find a certain few great questions of a completely stereotyped mould. And their stereotyped mould is a sign that these questions are inevitable and indispensable. They are always thrusting themselves forward afresh by a positive necessity, and even with the best of intentions they cannot be repulsed without subverting the life of the spirit as a whole.

What are these inescapable questions, then, which are so fundamental to the life of the spirit?

In the first place there is the theoretical question, or *the question of truth*. Its fundamental importance for the spiritual life is easily perceived if we try the intellectual experiment of excluding the notion of truth from the life of the spirit in order to see what remains. If there were no grounds for distinguishing between true and false, then all

25

research would be meaningless; it would be meaningless to try to refer any phenomenon to its causes; it would indeed be meaningless to make any statement or to think any thought, since a statement or a thought can only have meaning and significance if it claims to express a true relationship. At all events, the demand for consistency in thinking could not be maintained. It would be a matter of indifference whether we thought rightly or wrongly or did not think at all. It need hardly be said that that would mean the end of all that we understand by the life of the spirit. There have always been sceptics, of course, who have contested the legitimacy of the question of truth, but a consistent sceptic there has never been. Scepticism is by nature inconsistent. By his theory the sceptic disputes the legitimacy of the question of truth, yet the recognition of that question is the only condition on which his own theory can have any meaning. In other words, the sceptic stops his own mouth with his theory. The only consistent thing to do in such circumstances, would be to renounce all claim to spiritual life, and to return to that state of barbarism in which men had as yet no use for the distinction between true and false.

Alongside the question of truth we find a group of questions which can be summed up as *the ethical question*; and this is of equally fundamental importance for the spiritual life. It is the question of good and evil, and the closely related question of right and wrong. Here we are dealing with the foundation, not only of all social life, but also of individual character. Think away this foundation, and all real cultural and spiritual life will prove to be impossible. It is true that there is also an ethical scepticism which has attempted to get rid of ethical considerations, although this is far more rare than is usually supposed. Those who set up as immoralists and sceptics in the realm of ethics, often confine themselves to denying the validity of certain particular ethical precepts. Their criticism is directed against the ethical valuations of their time; and in this criticism they are sometimes well within their rights. But what gives force and conviction to their criticism is the fact that they themselves have an ethical ideal of which the prevalent ethical outlook falls short. Nevertheless, many such critics give the impression of being moral sceptics, simply because they confine themselves to criticism of the *status quo*. If only they were required to show what ethical principles they would put in the place of those they deny, it would become clear that theirs is no true scepticism. It is simply that one ethical view has come into conflict with another. But both views rest on the recognition that the ethical question as such is justified. Genuine ethical scepticism, on the other hand, disputes the legitimacy of the ethical question itself. It does not recognize the distinction between good and evil, and it rejects all ethical valuation no matter what its basic principles are. It is absolutely indifferent to the contrast between right and wrong, and it regards any consideration of human will and action from this point of view as illegitimate. Ethical scepticism has seldom been carried to this length, presumably because it is only too evident that such radical scepticism would entail the complete collapse of the spiritual life.

As a third question that is fundamental for the life of the spirit we may perhaps name at this point *the aesthetic question* concerning 'the beautiful' and 'the sublime'. It too is an all-embracing form of spiritual life, even if its inevitability and necessity are less easy to demonstrate, and even if aesthetic scepticism is more difficult to refute than theoretical or ethical scepticism.

These three questions, however, do not cover the whole range of the life of the spirit. A fourth and no less fundamental question is that of the eternal, which we recognize as *the religious question*. For it is precisely characteristic of religion that it claims to raise human life above this sensible, finite, temporal sphere to the sphere of the eternal. To look

27

at religion from any other point of view than this is to run into insuperable difficulties. If we try, for example, to subsume religion under a concept such as the idea of God, which in our view is essential to religion, we encounter the objection that there can be an atheistic religion, as witness original Buddhism. Or suppose we employ the now generally accepted 'idea of the holy' in attempting to describe the content of religion. From a psychological point of view there is no objection to that; but for our present purpose of locating religion within the life of the spirit, the idea of the holy suffers from the disadvantage of providing no clear picture of the place and significance of religion in the wider context of the spiritual life. Moreover, the idea of the holy itself is evidence in favour of the idea of the eternal as the basic factor in religion, since it can be included without difficulty as a subordinate element in the latter. On the other hand, there can be no legitimate objection to our using the question of the eternal as a periphrasis for religion when our purpose is to indicate its place within the life of the spirit. For it is impossible to see how religion would be possible without some relation to the eternal.

The necessary conditions for religion are lacking unless this present world of sense is set over against the world of eternity, and unless this life of ours is viewed *sub specie aeternitatis*, in the light of eternity. It need hardly be said that the idea of eternity as used here to indicate the basic factor in religion, has nothing to do with the popular notion of that which lies before and after time. Eternity is not an extension of time backwards and forwards, but an abolition and breaking through of time. It represents a life which knows that it is not subject merely to the conditions of finitude. It cannot therefore be simply identified with the eschatological 'world to come', nor has it primarily anything to do with the idea of 'life after death'. 'The religious man knows that he has a share in God's own life, and that he has it, not merely as being assured of it for a future existence, but precisely as a present possession. Religiousness reveals itself in the theoretical and practical awareness that the reality given in sensible experience is not the whole of reality, and that there is an eternal world. The eternal world, however, does not stand in such an exclusive relation to the temporal world in which we live, that we must leave this world behind before we can participate in the eternal. On the contrary, it is of the nature of piety to seek the traces of the eternal in everything that is and happens; and the stronger the piety is, the less it permits anything of the temporal to fall outside the world of eternity. The stronger it is, the more every moment of life becomes a religious moment, and the more everything in existence is viewed *sub specie aeternitatis.*' [1]

But is the question of the eternal really fundamental for the life of the spirit? Is it as inevitable and necessary, for example, as the question of truth or the ethical question? In other words, can we apply to it the principle: Think away the question of the eternal, and all real spiritual life will prove to be impossible?

The attempt to think away the question of the eternal is not merely a theoretical and intellectual experiment. It has been made often enough by the religious sceptics of all ages. But here also a word of caution is necessary. Much that goes by the name of scepticism in the realm of religion has nothing to do with real scepticism. Often it is the criticism of one religious view by another. *Alte dubitat qui altius credit*: He deeply doubts who more deeply believes. Yet even so, there is quite enough real religious scepticism both theoretical and practical. We are only concerned here with theoretical scepticism, and this is found above all in the so-called positivist conception of religion. According to this view, religion is not anything permanent in the life of the spirit, but something which both can and should disappear. It belongs to a stage of culture already superseded;

---

[1] A. Nygren, *Religiöst apriori* (1921), pp. 239–40.

it is merely a relic of that stage, and in due course will follow it into oblivion. Such a view reveals a singularly obscure and misleading notion of what religion is, inasmuch as it confuses religion with primitive world-view; but what rules it completely out of court is the fact that the question of the eternal can be shown to be so fundamental to the life of the spirit that the latter is impossible on any other basis.

We have already seen that the question of truth, the ethical question, and possibly the aesthetic question, each represent an inescapable presupposition of the life of the spirit. We can now relate these questions to that of the eternal by saying that none of these essential pillars of the spiritual life is able to stand by itself, but each must rest on the foundation of the question of the eternal. The justification for this assertion will be clear if we consider the following four indisputable facts.

(1) Common to all these fundamental questions is the fact that, each in its own way, they all claim to be valid. When we made a cognitive judgement, for example, it claims to be valid from the point of view of truth. The ethical judgement makes the same claim to validity from the point of view of morality. The validity which thus finds expression is characteristic of the life of the spirit.

(2) The idea of validity, however, contains a mostly unobserved but none the less inescapable presupposition. When we describe anything as valid, we do not mean that it is valid at a single point in space and time, or merely for one individual. We mean that it is valid without regard to space and time, and for all individuals without distinction. When we say that the law of contradiction, for instance, possesses unconditional validity, we cannot mean that while it is valid in the place where we are, there might be a place where the propositions 'A is B' and 'A is not B' would not contradict and cancel each other out. Nor do we mean that it is valid in our time, but that there might have been in the past, or may be in the future, a time when it would not

be valid. Even if there was a time when men had no notion
of the law of contradiction, the factual relation expressed
in it possessed full validity none the less. And it is equally
clear that the law of contradiction cannot be valid for some
individuals and not others. Its nature is such as to be valid
everywhere, always, and for all. The same is true of the
validity of the ethical judgement. To anyone who really
understands the idea of morality, its validity can never be
spatially, temporally, or individually limited. We may
readily admit that the content of the moral demand is dependent on spatial, temporal and individual circumstances,
and varies as these vary. What we must deny, however, is
that the actual distinction between good and evil could ever
in any circumstances be abolished. Its validity transcends
space, time, and individual. Without such a supra-spatial,
supra-temporal and supra-individual validity, the life of the
spirit as a whole would be an illusion; the question of truth
as well as the ethical and aesthetic questions would lose its
meaning.

(3) It must be duly observed, however, that this presupposition, on which the whole of the life of the spirit rests,
is not found actually realized in any of these spheres,
whether theoretical, ethical, or aesthetic. The only thing
we can say about them is that they need and postulate this
presupposition. They possess it merely as a necessary
assumption, and not as a realized fact within their purview.

(4) Only in religion with its question of the eternal is this
presupposition of the life of the spirit realized. If the place
occupied by religion in the life of the spirit were empty,
the life of the spirit itself would be impossible. It would
hang in the air, it would build upon a presupposition that
was realized nowhere. But religion as an independent experience possesses just what the rest of the life of the spirit
requires for its foundation. The peculiar characteristic of
religion, as we have said already, is that it raises human life
above everything sensible, finite, temporal, and individually

31

limited, and brings it into the realm of the eternal. In a word, the valid, eternal is the ultimate presupposition of the spiritual life, and religion is essentially experience of the eternal. To this extent we are justified in saying that the source of the life of the spirit is located in the realm of religion.

Our survey of the life of the spirit has shown that it is characterized by the validity which finds expression in it, and that it confronts us with certain comprehensive, necessary and inescapable questions, which represent different aspects, so to speak, of the spiritual life. These different aspects reciprocally condition one another. To make this reciprocity clearer by means of a simile, we may liken them to buttresses supporting and holding each other up. If one of them gives way, the whole building, the whole life of the spirit, collapses. Of chief importance, however, is religion, since the whole structure rests ultimately on the question of the eternal. No matter which of the other great questions of the spiritual life we take as our starting-point, if only we follow up its implications we always arrive finally at the question of the eternal—which proves the necessity and inevitability of that question. Thus we have located religion, so to speak; we have found its fixed point in the life of the spirit.

Our conclusion is further supported by the fact that these questions of the spiritual life have shown themselves capable of creating enduring social forms. The question of truth, the ethical question, the aesthetic question, and the question of the eternal are not merely ideal direction-posts for the spiritual life; they also embody themselves in very tangible, objective, outward forms of organization. The question of truth is the foundation of that extensive sociological organization which goes by the name of science; what we have summarily termed the ethical question lies at the basis of every ethical or legal society and the life of the state; the aesthetic question serves as a foundation for art, considered as an objective entity; and on the basis of the question of the eternal there arises the religious society and cult-community. Just as we can point out a person by pointing to his body, so with reference to the life of the spirit we can point to these organizations. They are, so to speak, the body of the spiritual life, its external, visible manifestation. It is true that there are various other sociological formations besides these; but not one bears the same stamp of necessity and inevitability which they have. The reason for this is not far to seek. The question of truth, the ethical question, the aesthetic question, and the question of the eternal are fundamental and necessary to the life of the spirit; therefore no merely private interest attaches to them, but a common interest of everybody. Neither science, morality, art nor religion can be described from this point of view as a 'private affair', any more than the life of the spirit in general can ever be cultivated as a private affair. Social formation and fellowship can occur, of course, where the promotion of more private interests is concerned; but when the interest ceases to be one which several hold in common, then the accidental motive for the formation of the society disappears, and the fellowship, too, comes to an end. Those forms of organization and of society, however, which are based on the life of the spirit, are not due to individual interests and incidental motives, but rather to motives which are necessary and essential to the spiritual life. Therefore the fellowship erected on their foundation acquires a certain trace of necessity and indissolubility. Here we find new proof of the fact already mentioned, that religion is the deepest and most fundamental thing in the life of the spirit. For it cannot be denied that as a force creative of social forms religion takes first place, both as regards its age and extent and as regards the elasticity and inwardness of the fellowship it produces.

By giving religion its necessary place in the life of the spirit we have at the same time brought to light three important facts.

First, it has become quite plain that any scepticism directed against religion is untenable. To regard existence from a religious point of view is not an arbitrary procedure with which we could equally well dispense. Religion is not something accidental which thrusts itself upon human life from without; it is the spiritual life itself in the deepest sense of the term. People who lack understanding of religion may regard it merely as a web of strange ritual practices, mythological notions and the like, cast over human life from outside, which we can and ought to shake off as quickly as possible. But that is obviously an illusion. The fact of the life of the spirit rests upon the fact of religion. Religion is thus shown to be a universally valid and necessary form of life. The validity of the religious question is demonstrated by exactly the same means, the only possible means, by which also the validity of scientific knowledge and the ethical relation can be demonstrated. No one who has clearly perceived the presuppositions upon which he himself lives, in so far as he has any part in the life of the spirit, can be indifferent to the religious question.

Secondly, we have learnt that religion is a unique and absolutely independent form of spiritual life. This follows directly from what has been said. If religion is a necessary and inevitable form of life, then it possesses something needful and indispensable for the life of the spirit, something not to be found in any of the other forms of life, so that none of them can take the place of religion and deputize for it. The philosophy of religion has often sinned against this principle. Kant, for example, who defines religion as 'the knowledge of all our duties as divine commands', plainly fails to preserve the specific nature of religion, and in particular to make it independent of morals. And when Hegel roundly declares, 'Philosophy itself is divine worship; it is religion. Philosophy is identical with religion', no argument is needed to show that both the specific nature and the independence of religion have suffered. These examples show how necessary it is for an understanding of the specific nature of religion that we should start from the question of the eternal. That question distinguishes religion from every other form of spiritual life, and we should go with it to religion itself in order to listen to its own testimony.

By the independence of religion we do not mean primarily its psychological independence of other aspects of the life of the spirit. To insist upon the independence of religion in that sense would in fact be both fruitless and questionable. The different aspects of the life of the spirit are so interlocked that we cannot very well draw any sharp psychological boundaries between them. But religion is independent in this sense, that it represents an entirely different value and interest from either science, morality, or art. No matter how many elements from these other spheres may enter into the religious life, they make no difference at all to the independence of religion; for religion has its own end to pursue, and follows its own course. It is independent because it does not derive the justification of its existence from elsewhere. Religion does not continue to exist because it is useful for science, for the moral life, or for art. It continues to exist because it itself possesses a question no less great and necessary and inevitable than theirs, the question of the eternal. Even if religion proved to be of no advantage to these other forms of life, and to have not the very least contribution to make to the problem of knowledge or ethics or aesthetics, this would in no way rob religion of its significance. Religion is not a mere means to other ends, but an end in itself. Religion does not live by the kind permission of others; it stands on its own ground and lives by the importance and inevitability of its own question, the question of the eternal.

35

The third point follows, therefore, that religion is an absolutely autonomous form of life. If we wish to understand it, we must see it as it grows on its own ground and in accordance with its own laws. In the study of religion this principle, too, has often been violated. An outstanding example is the attempt to construe religious development as parallel to the development of the general conception of the world, or actually as a consequence of it. Most people recognize that intellectual and ethical development do not necessarily go together; that keen intelligence and ethical deficiency can often exist side by side in the individual; and that an age of perfected intellectual culture can also be an age of ethical degeneration. But the notion is often cherished where religion is concerned, that its development can be understood simply as a consequence of general intellectual development. From this point of view the evolution of religion is conceived on something like the following lines. So long as thinking is incoherent and chaotic, religion is animistic or fetishistic, and is dominated by the idea of tabu and similar unenlightened notions. When thought is unable to embrace more than the present moment, it is paralleled by the religious stage which knows only 'gods of the moment'. When thinking, however, has reached such a maturity that, although it is still limited and particular, it embraces not merely the single moment and a single object, but a series of moments and a group of objects, then religion progresses to the stage of polytheism; the gods assume a definite character and have their limited sphere of influence, their special tasks, and so on. When, finally, thought becomes comprehensive and universal and embraces the whole of existence as a unity, polytheistic religion is no longer tenable. In religion, too, a comprehensive unity must be achieved; and religion progresses to its highest stage, monotheism. All this may sound plausible enough, but on closer examination we soon discover that it cannot be maintained. Are we really to believe that the monotheistic deist, whose

God is merely the Prime Mover, who set the world mechanism going at the beginning but is now so remote that a personal relationship with him is an impossibility, and anything in the nature of prayer is regarded as the veriest delusion—are we really to believe that this monotheistic deist stands religiously higher than the polytheist who lives in intimate fellowship with his gods? Is it not possible that even in the most primitive belief in tabu there is more real religion than its often quite extraordinary ideas might lead one to expect? Is it quite so certain that a monotheistic form of belief, just because it is monotheistic, must be admitted to stand higher than any and every polytheism? Yes, if it is regarded as a religious world-view; if it is regarded as religion, no. The difference is that in the former case we must employ a standard of measurement taken from scientific life; in the latter we must measure religion autonomously with a religious standard. Many forms of religion which stand lower down in the scale when regarded as world-views, take a higher place when we regard them from the autonomous point of view of religion and the question of the eternal; for they can show a more vigorous experience of the eternal than many a 'higher' religion.[2]

This last-named principle of the autonomy of religion means that religion obeys its own laws; that it can only be rightly understood and expounded from an essentially religious point of view; and that every attempt to construe the meaning of religion by the application of laws which govern other spheres of the spiritual life is bound to fail. It is this principle we shall have to apply in our next chapter, where we are to indicate some characteristic and essential features of religion in general.

[2] This general reflection does not conflict with the fact that we cannot give any scientifically demonstrable answer to the question of the relative worth of different religions, and that our attitude to these religions depends in the last resort upon personal decision. On this point see A. Nygren: *Dogmatikens vetenskapliga grundläggning* (1922), pp. 36–42.

THREE

Religion

B Y SHOWING the question of the eternal to be inevitable and fundamental for the life of the spirit, we have discovered the necessary place of religion within that life. We have found the fixed point with which all that can be called religion is connected, and so have proved that religion is not an alien, arbitrary, and accidental thing due to merely external causes and unable to touch the deepest depths of human life.

We must note, however, that the fixed point we have found is not the same thing as the essence of religion; it is not that permanent element or distinctive character of religion which we are seeking. This fixed point, the question of the eternal, is rather like an abstraction from the essence of religion, although we have not arrived at it by the method of abstraction. It is not a substitute for the essence of religion, but it will be of invaluable assistance to us in our search for that essence. It is the compass, so to speak, which is to guide and direct us when we venture into the infinitely varied realm of religion. The inevitability and necessity of the question of the eternal are our guarantee that we are not in error, and that in religion we are not dealing with a deceptive phantom. They show that it is not merely accidental that everything in the world of religion can be subsumed under the question of the eternal. But the forms which religion will assume in any particular instance cannot be determined in advance; we must go with our question to the world of religion and obtain purely empirical evidence. Some would perhaps recommend a different procedure, and suggest a logical analysis of the idea of the eternal as a means of discovering the basic forms of all religion. But this is impossible, because, as we have already shown, religion must be treated as autonomous; it must be treated in accordance with its own laws, and cannot be constructed by logical method. What this method produces has very little to do with real religion. We can only do justice to the autonomy of religion if we go with our question to the actually given religions, and let their testimony decide what content is to be put into the question of the eternal.

With the thought of the eternal as our lodestar when we travel through the history of religions in different ages and circumstances, we do not find, as has often been supposed, an unbroken development from the lowest to the highest forms of religion, from primitive religion to complete 'ethical monotheism'. Yet it is not difficult to see that the question of the eternal occurs everywhere in certain more or less constant forms. These may be summarized in the following four points.

(1) Wherever religion is found at all, it claims to unveil the eternal for us. There are religions which lack one or another element which we normally regard as inseparable from religion; there are even religions that lack any idea of God. But there is no religion which does not claim to be revelation, the revelation of the eternal in this world of time. On this point there is no difference between the different kinds of religiosity. We speak, and rightly speak, of 'revealed religion' as a special kind in itself; and this might suggest that the idea of revelation were not a universal phenomenon of religion. But that is by no means so. A religion which lives solely within the world of sense and has no other terms of reference is no religion. All religion claims to be revelation in the sense that it claims to reveal an otherwise unknown world of eternity. Not least is this true of mysticism, which seeks to escape entirely from the sense world and to live its life in the infinite and eternal. Revelation is the characteristic word of all religion, whether

what is revealed is named God, the Eternal, or (impersonally) the eternal, the infinite, the ineffable—and whether the revelation of the eternal is found in something encountered from without, or in one's own inner self. Real religion is never merely abstract. It belongs to the sphere of the question of the eternal; yet it is not simply a matter of an idea of the eternal, where the eternal is treated merely as an abstract idea. Real religion is always concrete, and in it the eternal is found as the content of actual experience. It is never satisfied with the general conception of an 'eternal' underlying or concealed behind the texture of the sense world, but it seeks to discover this eternal itself in perceptible phenomena or experiences. That is why we can observe in the history of religion how men will find the eternal revealed and embodied in fetishes, images, incarnations and so on. Even in mysticism, which rejects all outward and tangible forms for the eternal, men seek to grasp the eternal in entirely palpable and concrete inner experiences. It is this fact which distinguishes religious mysticism from philosophical.

Religion is essentially relevation of the eternal, experience of the eternal. Where the Eternal or the eternal is not in any way met or experienced, we have no right to speak of religion.

(2) The second characteristic feature of all religion is what we might call the seriousness, the disquiet, the judgement of the eternal. The experience of the eternal is universally accompanied by a seriousness and gravity which distinguishes it from all else. William James is right when he says that one of the most essential characteristics of religion is that it is always a serious state of the soul. "There must be something solemn, serious, and tender about any attitude which we denominate religious.' 'The divine shall mean for us only such a primal reality as the individual feels impelled to respond to solemnly and gravely.' [1] The history

---

[1] *The Varieties of Religious Experience*, p. 38.

of religion contains the most eloquent and convincing testimony that this is the case.

Even the primitive mind has a distinct sense of the seriousness and gravity of the experience of the eternal. This is very evident in the disquiet which finds expression, for example, in the idea of tabu. The eternal is not a plaything; it is dangerous to come too near it. Whatever in any way bears the marks of the eternal, or is at all closely related to it, is filled with mysterious power which can have disastrous effects on anyone who has the temerity to approach it.

What finds expression of this kind on the lowest level, expresses itself at a higher stage as a feeling of disquiet, responsibility, and judgement in the presence of the eternal. A typical example of this is the scene in the sixth chapter of Isaiah. In the temple the prophet is permitted to see the glory of the Lord; the veil is momentarily drawn aside from the eternal world. His immediate reaction to this is the recognition of his own uncleanness and unworthiness, his sin and iniquity. 'Woe is me! for I am undone; because I am a man of unclean lips, and I dwell in the midst of a people of unclean lips: for mine eyes have seen the King, the Lord of hosts.' The light from the experience of the eternal falls like a lightning flash over an existence not conditioned by the eternal, and becomes a judgement upon it.

The experience of the eternal is bound, in the nature of the case, to produce a reaction of this kind. As long as the world of sense is the only world a man takes into account, his life is relatively tranquil. But when he suddenly finds himself confronted by the eternal, and a new world is disclosed to him, his whole existence is inevitably set a-quaking. New and unimagined possibilities are now presented to him as reality. The experience of the eternal begets the disquiet of the eternal; it sheds a deep seriousness over life; it vastly increases the sense of the responsibility of life; and it becomes, finally, a judgement upon life. So long as we

41

know nothing but sensible reality, naturally we cannot measure anything except by its standards. But when the experience of the eternal has brought a new reality, the old criteria can no longer be applied. The great transvaluation of all values begins, compared with which all other transvaluations, though made with such grand gestures and so naïve an exaggeration of their importance, prove to be mere child's play. Thorough as these other transvaluations may be, they never mean more than the transference of emphasis from one point in everyday experience to another. By this means we obtain no really new light, no really deep and radical transvaluation with sufficient vitality and force to transform our manner of life. The highest we can attain by the purely 'this-worldly' approach is the rather mythological idea of our responsibility to the principle of evolution or to generations yet unborn. But the experience of the eternal begets the sense of unconditional responsibility, eternal responsibility; and it is not merely responsibility in view of something future, but it is such that every moment of life has eternal content. It is then that the consciousness of sin and unworthiness arises. In the light of the eternal or the Eternal, which comprises in itself all that can be called 'worth', man is bound to become conscious of the unworthiness of his own existence.

It might perhaps be objected that the above argument is too much influenced by the prophetic type of piety with its ethical seriousness, its highly developed consciousness of sin, and its disquiet in face of the eternal. These things, it might be thought, play no essential part in mysticism, for example. The objection, however, cannot be maintained. It may be true that the disquiet and the consciousness of sin, as we normally understand it, do not play a very great part in mysticism; but what we are talking about here is found in mysticism as much as anywhere else, though it appears there in a specially modified form. Why is it that the mystic looks down upon the whole of sensible reality with such sovereign contempt? It is simply because the eternal world has cast its shadow over sensible existence, and revealed its unworthiness and nothingness. Here, if anywhere, we can speak of the judgement of the eternal upon the temporal. Here, if anywhere, we see the power which the experience of the eternal possesses to effect a transvaluation of all values. So this, too, is an element in the essence of all religion. Where the question of the eternal is merely employed for speculative purposes, as an object for the activity of thought; where the experience of the eternal is not allowed to prove itself a mighty reality by evoking in some way the seriousness, the disquiet, the responsibility, the judgement of the eternal; then we have no right to speak of religion.

(3) A third characteristic feature of all religion is discovered when we notice how the two points already described and the tension they produce require with a certain positive necessity that a further step should be taken. We started with the revelation of the eternal; but this has become the judgement of the eternal. 'The glory of the Lord' reveals the miserable plight of man. The holiness of the Lord becomes the judgement on man's sin. The 'wrath of God', the Eternal as a consuming fire—this and this alone seems to result from the two aspects of religion which we have so far described. No man can see the Eternal and live!

Religion, however, seeks to overcome the tension it has itself created. It seeks to effect a kind of *modus vivendi* between the Eternal and corruptible man, between the Holy and the sinner. It seeks to build a bridge between the two; it seeks to bring something which can, as it were, cover up human unworthiness and wretchedness. It seeks to indicate ways and means for the covering of sin. And here we come to that whole complex in the history of religion which can be described by the words: purifications, means of atonement, atoning sacrifices. Even if external means of atone-

43

ment play a relatively small part in certain kinds of religion, especially in mystical types, this does not contradict our statement that we have here something distinctive of all religion. What we are discussing here is found in mysticism no less than in other forms of religion, although in mysticism the sacrifice is 'inward' and not external. Mysticism knows no other way to communion and union with the eternal than that which leads through purification. 'Purification' is usually the first stage on the way of the mystic, without which he cannot come into contact with the eternal. A religion which did not claim to make possible the meeting between the eternal and man, a religion which did not claim to be the bridge over an otherwise impassable gulf, would be a monstrosity.

For man to be able to enter into fellowship with the eternal and the divine, an atonement, a purification, a covering of his unworthiness is necessary. Man's life must acquire something of the quality of eternity. The history of religion shows that this can be sought in two opposite directions. Either purification proceeds from man's side, or else the covering, the atonement and the purification are conceived as proceeding from the eternal and the divine itself. (i) For the ordinary, uninitiated man the eternal is a consuming fire, an annihilating force. Therefore the question arises, what rites and purifications, what observances and works will enable man to enter into a positive relationship with the eternal, either on particular occasions or permanently. What precautions are necessary in order for man to associate with the eternal without danger? (ii) The second idea is one which is found at all stages of religion, from the most primitive to the highest religious levels. There is something like it even in certain forms of tabuism. Primitive man knows instinctively, without premeditation and calculation, that he can safely approach and utilize for his own ends the mysterious power of the tabu-object only if he himself is in possession of a power that is akin to it.

44

That is to say, he must himself be more or less tabu. In order to get into this condition certain initiations are necessary; and primitive man is aware that as far as these are concerned the initiative belongs to that which is filled with power, that which bears the marks of the eternal. No observances of any kind resting on the basis of 'ordinary' life can make man fit to have intercourse with the eternal. A similar awareness that purification must proceed from the Eternal is found is the sixth chapter of Isaiah, quoted above. In the presence of the glory of the Lord the prophet realizes his own unworthiness and impurity, and then the narrative continues: 'Then flew one of the seraphim unto me, having a live coal in his hand, which he had taken with the tongs from off the altar; and he touched my mouth with it, and said, Lo, this hath touched thy lips; and thine iniquity is taken away, and thy sin purged.' The coal that could cleanse had to be taken from the altar; the atonement had to come from the Lord. Man's own conformity to the eternal, attained by himself, can never cover human unworthiness; only an atonement and a purification given by the Lord can do this. Here one of the profoundest ideas of religion has found clear expression.

Now let us consider these two ways of purification and atonement in the light of our principle concerning the autonomy of religion; and let us try to see which of them fares the better when tested by the logic of religion itself. There can scarcely be any doubt that the second of the two represents the deeper religious idea. We must be quite clear, however, what the question at issue really is. Human unworthiness is here set over against the absolute worth of the eternal. In the light of eternity everything human, everything not determined by eternity, is shown to be sheer unworth, sheer nonentity and a thing of nought. In that case, to expect purification and atonement from human observances and works is a contradiction in terms. How can human unworth be covered by piling unworth on unworth?

Can we make it more worthy in this way? Can we really reach infinity by adding nought to nought? Therefore it is from the Eternal Himself that the purification, the covering and the atonement must come to enable man to have intercourse with the Eternal. This is religion's last word on that question.

(4) We now come to the fourth characteristic feature of all religion. Religion claims to be real, vital fellowship and union between the eternal and man; it seeks to infuse a divine life into man. The eternal and the temporal, the divine and the human, are not to stand side by side as two parties still fundamentally alien to one another, once they have been reconciled and are able to meet without serious discord on the basis of the *modus vivendi* that has been established. Man and the eternal must not remain as opposites; they must not stand over against each other as two impenetrables. All genuine religion claims to be real and vital fellowship with the divine, a permeation of the whole of human life by the divine. The in-dwelling of God in the soul, the union of the soul with God—this is the aim of religion. This is the point of view from which we must regard that whole series of religious phenomena which includes both the primitive view that man can attain union with the divine by eating the deity itself, and also the sublimest mysticism, in which the contrast between man and the eternal-infinite-ineffable-divine has ceased to exist, and nothing less than a complete identification of God and man is sought. In the primitive totemistic sacrament, where man eats the totem animal he worships; in the slaying and eating of their god by the Mexican Aztecs; in the Dionysiac orgies, where men fall in a wild delirium upon the goat dedicated to Dionysius, rend it in pieces and devour it; in the sacred dances; in the ecstatic conditions; in the mysticism of both East and West, with its various stages of absorption and its manifold refinements of bodily and spiritual *exercitia*;—in all these there is concealed a kindred

religious motive, the need for perfect union with God and complete permeation by the divine. Granted that these motives often appear in such a crude garb that it is difficult to recognize a legitimate religious need in them; nevertheless the unequivocal testimony of these and similar phenomena is that in the human spirit from its most primitive beginnings there dwells an ineradicable urge to take the eternal into itself, to become one with the divine, to be permeated and upborne by a new and eternal life.

This striving for a vital fellowship and union with the eternal has found its most vigorous expression in mysticism, but it is not distinctive of mysticism alone; it is a feature which belongs to all real and genuine religion. It is true that in other forms of religion, where this element is held in balance with the three preceding elements, man is clearly aware of the distance between the human and the divine, and therefore abstains from an over-hasty identification of them; yet his goal is always union with the divine. Where the relationship between the human and the divine is one of contrast and opposition alone, without any union or vital fellowship, we have no right to speak of religion.

In the above four points we have indicated what we must consider as the essential and permanent structure of religion, the structure which is found more or less in all the phenomena which we have a right to call religion. We may now briefly summarize the conclusions we have so far reached.

Religion is an essential and integral part of the life of the human spirit. It represents that aspect of the life of the spirit which is expressed in the question of the eternal. To ignore this question is to rob the spiritual life of the only foundation on which it can be built up. Religion thus provides the foundation for all spiritual life. At the same time, it possesses over against this its complete independence and its own specific character. Religion represents a completely different interest from any other form of life. All attempts to reduce religion to something else which is not originally religion—whether it be science, morality, art or anything else—is doomed to failure in advance. It is equally impossible to understand religion aright, if we merely try to reconstruct it by the aid of such points of view and ideas as we have gained in non-religious experience. We must let religion itself tell us what religion is. We must learn the content of the question of the eternal by noticing how it actually appears in the historically given religions. In a word, religion is autonomous, and therefore it can be rightly understood and evaluated only from its own point of view.

Finally, we find that religion constantly appears under four aspects: (1) Religion is revelation of the eternal; it is concrete experience of the eternal. (2) Religion is awareness of the infinite gulf which separates the self-revealing divine from the human; it is the seriousness, the disquiet, the judgement of the eternal. (3) Religion is the bridging of this gulf; it is reconciliation between the eternal, the worthy, and human unworthiness, the reconciliation of the holy and the sinner, the divine and the human. (4) Religion is man's vital fellowship and union with the Eternal; it is the permeation of human life by divine, eternal life.

FOUR

Christianity

AFTER HAVING outlined the essential elements of all religion we now go on to ask what it is that specially distinguishes Christianity from all other religions. First, however,
there is an important observation to be made. In this
inquiry about the distinctive marks of Christianity we do
not propose to add to the four points already made, which
indicate what is common to all religion, a further series of
points purporting to contain the exclusive properties of
Christianity. Different religions are not related to one
another in such a way that they have a certain number of
things in common and others not. It is rather the case that
Christianity displays at every point the marks which distinguish it from all other religions. In describing the distinctive marks of Christianity, therefore, we must take the
four points indicated above, and inquire what special content is given to each of them in Christianity. Then we shall
see that Schleiermacher was not far wrong in his famous
definition, when he said that 'Christianity is essentially dis-
tinguished from other faiths by the fact that everything in
it is related to the redemption accomplished by Jesus of
Nazareth.' [1] Suppose we wish to state in brief what the
essential thing in Christianity is, the thing that distinguishes it absolutely from all other religions and gives it its
specific character: we cannot quote one or more articles of
doctrine, but can only point to that Person who stands at
the centre of Christianity, and sets his own seal on everything in it. 'It is evident that Christianity and Christ are
most intimately connected with one another. It has been

[1] *The Christian Faith* (trans. by J. Baillie, 1922), p. 9.

so from the beginning. As far back as we can trace Christianity, Christ stands at its centre. And the same is true of the history of Christianity to the present day. There may have been varied ideas about the nature of that connection. It has been conceived in more strict and less strict terms; it has been thought of as inward and deep, or as rather external and mechanical. But the bond cannot be broken. Christ and Christianity have grown together indissolubly. It is impossible to separate Christianity from Christ without disrupting it and robbing it of its uniqueness.' [2]

The central importance of Christ for Christianity is plainest of all when we consider Christianity under the four aspects which we found to be distinctive of all religion whatsoever.

(1) First we may ask: Where does Christianity find the revelation of the eternal? Where in this world does the Christian experience the breaking in of eternity? The answer cannot be other than this: In Jesus Christ. In Him the Christian faith has always seen 'the effulgence of God's glory, and the very image of his substance' (Heb 1[3]). In the person of Jesus, as nowhere else, Christianity finds the Eternal Himself revealed in time. This in no way means that Jesus alone, as an isolated fact, is the only revelation of God. On the contrary, the Christian finds traces of God everywhere in the universe. But of all the other things that may be a revelation of God to us we can say, as was once said of nature: 'One who is already religious finds God in nature; but no one becomes religious by its means.' [3] It is Christ who has opened our eyes to the eternal world; and it is therefore no exaggeration to say that without Him we have no God. Without Him we might perhaps possess some conception of God, or even a well-defined idea of God. But religion is not the same thing as a conception or idea of God. As we have seen, religion presupposes a

[2] G. Aulen: *Våra tankar om Kristus* (1921), p. 3.

[3] W. Herrmann.

palpable revelation of the eternal, an entirely concrete experience of God; and that is what Christianity finds in Jesus Christ. The Christian can find something of the revelation of God in other things, as we have said; and this, too, means an entirely concrete experience of God. But in these things the Christian only finds traces of God; in Christ he sees the countenance and very heart of God revealed. When the Christian believes in God's love, for example, he does not so believe because he has thought it all out, and come to the conclusion on speculative grounds that God can only be conceived in this way, or that the abstract idea of God would be degraded and inconsistent without this attribute. The Christian believes in God's love because he has seen this love shine forth with entirely concrete features in Jesus Christ. What God is like, what God's ultimate will is—these things the Christian learns to understand only by looking at Jesus.

Christ is the place where the eternal breaks in, He is the concrete revelation of God for us; and it is just because He occupies such a central place that Christianity takes its name from Him, and we as Christians bear His name. Where Christ does not occupy this place as the revelation of the eternal, we have, strictly speaking, no justification for talking about Christianity. There are some schools of thought which largely accept and adopt the moral requirements of Jesus, for example, and yet protest against being described as Christians. They are quite right to protest. All we can say is that certain ethical ideas of Christianity have won acceptance even outside the strictly Christian sphere. In its inmost essence Christianity is neither ethical ideas nor, indeed, any kind of mere 'ideas'. Christianity is a religious reality and as such it is primarily concerned with the question of the eternal and the breaking in of eternity into time. In cases where this religious question is not a live issue, or where the satisfaction of this need is found elsewhere than in Christ, we ought for the sake of clarity to avoid using the word Christianity. We have before us, then, a characteristic feature of all Christianity. And it is no mere accident, therefore, that this revelational significance of Christ is stressed everywhere in the New Testament—in the Synoptic Gospels no less than in the Pauline and Johannine writings: 'Neither doth any know the Father, save the Son, and he to whomsoever the Son willeth to reveal him' (Mt 11²⁷): 'The light of the knowledge of the glory of God in the face of Jesus Christ' (2 Cor 4⁶): 'He that hath seen me hath seen the Father' (Jn 14⁹).

(2) Secondly we may ask: Where does Christianity find the seriousness, the disquiet, the judgement of the eternal? The answer is again: In Jesus Christ. It is in Him that the eternal and the divine breaks forth with its full force. That is why Christians of all ages, when confronted with Him, have had an experience similar to that of the prophet Isaiah in the temple when he saw the glory of the Lord. In the presence of the majesty and glory, the purity and power of Jesus, no man still in possession of his sight can avoid passing judgement on himself and on his life. We have evidence of this on every hand. A woman, who has stood before His heart-searching glance for only a few moments, says: 'Come, see a man, which told me all things that ever I did: can this be the Christ?' (Jn 4²⁹). The centurion at Capernaum confesses: 'I am not worthy that thou shouldest come under my roof' (Lk 7⁶). And it is related of one of His disciples: 'Simon Peter fell down at Jesus' knees, saying, Depart from me; for I am a sinful man, O Lord' (Lk 5⁸). In every case we have the expression of an unreflecting, instinctive sense of personal unworthiness and personal sinfulness; and this sense was aroused by the impression these people had that they were in the presence of the Holy and the Transcendent. Such examples could easily be multiplied throughout the whole history of Christianity.

As a further illustration of the transvaluation of all values which is effected by the experience of the eternal in the presence of Christ, we may notice the case of St Paul. He had lived according to the strictest ethical standards that were anywhere to be found among his people and in his age. Judged by these standards he was irreproachably righteous; that was his glory and renown. Then came his experience of the eternal on the Damascus road, in the light of which his whole system of values assumed an entirely different aspect from before. Hence, years later, after describing the things he had previously regarded as the highest values, things in which he had gloried, he could write: 'Howbeit what things were gain to me, these have I counted loss for Christ' (Phil 3⁷).

What happened to Paul was simply what happens on every occasion when the eternal discloses itself to man. The disclosure is at the same time a revelation of the unworthiness of man's whole existence. It is not, however, the same thing as we experience in the light of our own ideal. We may experience our unworthiness in looking at this, too, when we realize how far we still are from its attainment; but then we can at least say that we are on the right path. The goal may be infinitely remote, yet it is at the end of the road we are travelling. But in the light of the revelation of the eternal, as Paul's example shows, we are challenged to a complete reversal of our way, a thorough transvaluation of all our values. Our previous ideal itself is shattered, an ideal we have constructed on the basis of our ordinary mundane consciousness. In the light of our new experiences the ideal itself cannot be maintained any longer. As long as we are unaware that there exists anything to be taken into account beyond what is contained within the limits of temporal existence, we have no occasion to seek any other ideal than that which is based upon temporal existence. But when the experience of the eternal takes place, this ideal falls to the ground, destroyed by our widened experience; and with it must fall the entire system of valuations based upon it.

53

This transvaluation of all values is quite typical of the Christian's experience of the eternal in the presence of Christ. The Pharisaic standpoint of Paul before his experience on the Damascus road was of that lofty type which deserves the name of ethical idealism; yet it was this very thing that was destroyed by his meeting with Christ. For in fact Christianity is something quite different from ethical idealism. Ethical idealism is characterized by a certain sense of quiet security born of the consciousness that one is moving along the lines of the ethical will; it possesses a certain consciousness of one's own superior worth as an autonomous and self-legislating ethical subject. Now Christianity, too, knows of a quiet security; but that is never the first thing in Christianity. Christianity is in the first instance the disquiet evoked by the eternal in the presence of Christ. To know Christ is to know judgement passed on oneself; to know Christ is to know oneself a miserable sinner.

(3) Thirdly we ask: Where does Christianity find the solution of this deep conflict between the Eternal and human unworthiness, between the Holy and the sinner? Again the answer is: In Jesus Christ. A characteristic feature of all that can be called Christianity is that in Christ a man experiences not merely judgement, but also restoration; his sin is not merely discovered, but also covered up. Rudolf Otto has an apt word to say about this: 'No religion has brought the mystery of the need for atonement or expiation to so complete, so profound, or so powerful expression as Christianity. . . . This atonement mystery is a "moment" which no Christian teaching that purports to represent the religious experience of the Christian and biblical tradition can afford to surrender. The teacher will have to make explicit, by an analysis of the Christian religious experience, how the "very numen", by imparting itself to the worshipper, becomes itself the means of "atonement". And in this regard it does not matter so very much

what the decisions of the commentators are as to what, if anything, Paul or Peter wrote on the subject of expiation and atonement, or whether, indeed, there is any "scriptural authority" for the thing at all. Were there in Scripture no word written about it, it might still be written today from our own experience. But it would indeed be extraordinary if it had not long ago been written of. For the God of the New Testament is not less holy than the God of the Old Testament, but more holy. The interval between the creature and Him is not diminished but made absolute; the unworthiness of the profane in contrast to Him is not extenuated but enhanced. That God none the less admits access to Himself and intimacy with Himself is not a mere matter of course; it is a grace beyond our power to apprehend, a prodigious paradox. To take this paradox out of Christianity is to make it shallow and superficial beyond recognition. But if this is so, the intuitions concerning, and the need felt for, "Covering" and "Atonement" result immediately. And the divinely appointed means of God's self-revelation, where experienced and appraised as such—"the Word", "The Spirit", "the Person of Christ",—become that to which the man "flees", in which he finds refuge, and in which he "locks" himself, in order that, consecrated and cleansed of his "profaneness" thereby, he may come into the presence of Holiness itself.' [4]

The very essence of Christianity is atonement, reconciliation, the forgiveness of sins. In this the initiative lies wholly with God. 'All things are of God, who reconciled us to himself through Christ. . . . God was in Christ reconciling the world unto himself' (2 Cor 5$^{18-19}$). 'Jesus Christ is the propitiation for our sins; and not for ours only, but also for the whole world' (1 Jn 2^2). This is inseparable from Christian faith; if it were taken away, there would be no Christianity left. The various so-called theories of atonement attempt to explain this situation, each in its own way; but what we are

[4] *The Idea of the Holy* (1931), pp. 58-9.

concerned with here is not explanation but the fact that Christianity always finds its *modus vivendi* (if we may again use the term) between the Holy and the sinner in Christ alone. He furnishes the possibility for God and man to meet.

(4) Fourthly and finally: Where does Christianity find man's vital fellowship and union with God? In Jesus Christ. The ultimate concern of all religion is to deliver man from that state in which his own self is the centre of his life. It is to this end that religions confront us with their revelation of the eternal. So long as man only has to reckon with the world of time and sense, he cannot possibly find any other centre that is able successfully to join issue with this self-centre. But the egocentric disposition is the quint-essence of irreligion; and it is egocentricity which religion must regard as its chief task to eradicate. When the eternal discloses itself to man, it throws new and unexpected centres of value into the struggle; the disquiet evoked by the eternal renders man's habitual self-centre tottering and insecure; the judgement of the eternal reveals its unworthi-ness and fundamentally disqualifies it as a centre of value. The conclusion of the process is only reached when a new centre, derived from the sphere of the eternal, takes the place of the old and dominates man's life. That is what the mystic endeavours to achieve when he seeks by means of asceticism and ecstasy and other spiritual exercises to mortify the self; he seeks final deliverance from the narrow limitations of the self, in order to become one with the infinite and eternal. But the Christian possesses all this in Jesus Christ. Through its relationship to Him the self loses its egocentric character without having to be annihilated in the process—in accordance with the profound saying in Matthew 10: 'He that loseth his life for my sake shall find it'. There is an idea characteristic of all Christianity, which we may express thus: Christ is the life of Christians, and Christians are thereby united with God and share in His

eternal life. From this point of view a Christian is one whose life centre is not his own self but Christ; one who knows himself to be impelled and dominated by Christ and His Spirit. There has been discussion of Christ-mysticism in Paul, and we could also say that a certain kind of Christ-mysticism is inseparable from all that can be called Christianity. This change in the life centre finds expression in the progressive deliverance of the Christian's life from narrow self-determination. The self which insists on being at the centre of existence usurps the place that belongs to the Lord alone; and for Christianity this is the fundamental form of sin. It is overcome when the self is not only removed from the centre, so that it loses the right to dominate existence, but when the self ceases to have any right even to itself. 'Know ye not that ye are not your own?' (1 Cor 6^{19}). In its place another power comes to dominate life. 'For the love of Christ constraineth us; . . . and he died for all, that they which live should no longer live unto themselves, but unto him who for their sakes died and rose again. . . . Wherefore if any man is in Christ he is a new creature' (2 Cor 5$^{14-15, 17}$). It is therefore something distinctive not merely of Paul but of all Christianity, when he says: 'I live; and yet no longer I, but Christ liveth in me' (Gal 2^{20}).

When we contemplate the innumerable forms of Christianity both past and present, we ask: Is there anything permanent amid all this change? And we can now give our answer in the words of the New Testament: 'Jesus Christ is the same yesterday and today, yea and for ever' (Heb 13^8). He is the permanent element in Christianity; He is the central, the essential thing, the thing which sets its seal upon everything. Jesus Christ is the revelation of the Eternal in the world; the judgement of the Eternal upon the world; the atonement and reconciliation; and the divine Spirit at work in the world.

57

It is a matter of long-standing dispute, whether we should primarily be guided by 'the teaching of Jesus', when we try to determine the essence of Christianity, or by 'the teaching about Christ' which soon began to develop in the first Christian community. Cast in a less intellectualistic mould, the question has also been expressed thus: Is Christianity the same as the Gospel proclaimed by Jesus, or is it the Gospel about Christ, is Christ its object? What does it mean to be a Christian? Is it the same as having 'the faith of Jesus', that is, a faith in God like His; or does it mean having 'faith in Christ'? In other words, is Jesus Himself part of the Gospel, or was He simply the first to proclaim it? This question has also been linked with the problem of the relation of the Synoptic portrait of Jesus to the Pauline and Johannine picture of Christ. Which of these, it has been asked, is normative for Christianity? Are we to hold to the portrait of the historical Jesus which we find in the Synoptic gospels, or to the dogmatic picture of Christ in the Pauline and Johannine writings?

The preceding discussion should have made it clear that we have no use in our context for a contrast of this sort. Christianity is neither 'the teaching of Jesus' nor a 'teaching about Christ'. Only an intellectualistic conception of Christianity can be satisfied with such an alternative. And to oppose 'the Gospel of Jesus' to 'the Gospel about Christ', or 'the faith of Jesus' to 'faith in Christ', gives equally little help towards an understanding of Christianity. *Christianity is the question of the eternal as it finds its solution in Jesus Christ.* Christianity is the concrete experience, given in Jesus Christ, of the eternal in its various aspects. To be a Christian, therefore, means that one has met the eternal in Jesus Christ; that in His light one has experienced the judgement of eternity upon one's whole existence; that one is nevertheless able to approach the Eternal; and that one possesses His Spirit as the new centre and governing principle of one's life. The above-mentioned alternatives, therefore, are inapplicable, since the whole question has been raised to a different level. They are, in fact, no longer mutually exclusive, but have been brought together; and this finds external expression in our constant use of the formula 'Jesus Christ'. 'Jesus' signifies the historical fact with which Christianity is connected; 'Christ' represents the religious elaboration of this fact. Both are equally necessary and inevitable for Christianity. Often, however, people have wished to be content with only one of them. One line of argument has run as follows. The historical person of Jesus was early made the subject of pious speculation, and it soon became overgrown with all kinds of dogmatic notions such as are expressed in the conception of the Messiah-Christ, the idea of the Logos, and so forth. The picture of Jesus has suffered a fate similar to that of old paintings in churches, which at a later time were plastered over. The concrete human features have been enveloped in an abstract divine glory. What we must now do is to set the figure of Jesus free from this covering, and remove all the dogmatic elaborations, so that it may be seen as it historically was. Faith may then seek to derive what support and strength it can from this historical human life. An opposite line of argument presents us with a conception for which the person of Jesus as an historical fact means practically nothing at all, whilst Jesus as Christ-principle means everything.

A good deal can be said in justification of the former of the two conceptions just outlined. No one could fail to see that it is no mere recital of historical facts when the historical person of Jesus is set forth as the expected Messiah, the exalted Lord, the Logos of God, and so on. No one could fail to see that these are interpretations and 'elaborations' of an historical fact, and that they certainly cannot be described as purely historical. Yet it by no means follows from this that we ought to expurgate all 'elaborations' and only retain the purely historical picture of Jesus. Christianity is

59

never interested in Jesus simply as an historical person. What gives this person so decisive a significance is that in Him Christianity has found eternity breaking through. To this extent it is right to assert 'that the historical Jesus has never been, and in the nature of the case cannot be, the object of faith'. For it is not an historically demonstrable fact that eternity really breaks through in Him. That is already a religious elaboration of the historical fact which we have in the person of Jesus. On the other hand, it does not follow that Christianity is indifferent to the historical person of Jesus, like the second of the two views mentioned above. Both sides are equally essential for Christianity; both the historical fact of the person of Jesus and the religious elaboration and interpretation of that fact. Christianity is the synthesis of these two sides. When these two elements meet and unite in a single experience, when the disciples of Jesus have Him before their eyes as a concrete human person, and at the same time become convinced that in this person eternity has broken in upon them—in that hour Christianity is born. As long as they had only His words, His teaching, His example, His faith in God, there was still no new religion. He was only one teacher among others, greater than they perhaps, yet still only a teacher. He could lead them to a better understanding of the revelation of God which they already possessed, but He could not give them anything essentially new. The autonomous nature of religion—that is, the fact that it obeys its own laws, and is not tied to the apron-strings of the human intellect—is shown by the very fact that in the realm of religion nothing really new is ever produuced by the acquisition of new religious conceptions, or of a clearer and loftier idea of God. It is only through an experience of the eternal that anything new can come into being in this sphere; that is, only when the eternal and divine breaks through at a new point, and is grasped in a religious experience as just such an intrusion. The new religion, Christianity, had come into being when

the disciples could confess concerning the historical person
of Jesus, 'Thou art the Christ, the Son of the living God'
(Mt 16[16]), and could assert: 'God hath made him both
Lord and Christ, this Jesus whom ye crucified' (Acts 2[36]).
They had found a new religious centre. In the world in
which they lived they had found a point at which the world
of eternity met them.

That was what they sought to express by such syntheses
as, 'Jesus is Messiah', 'Jesus is Christ', 'Jesus is the Son of
God'. Now we can understand the significance of all the
names given to Jesus in the New Testament; names like
Christ, Messiah, the Lord (Kyrios), the Holy One of God,
the Son, the Son of Man, the Logos, and so on; names on
which future dogmatic construction could be based. They
are all different attempts to express the fundamental experience on which the whole of Christianity rests; they are
attempts to express the fact that in Jesus the disciples had
found the revelation of the eternal, the judgement of the
eternal, reconciliation with the Eternal, and perfect fellowship with God and unity with God.

It is therefore no mere accident that we know of no form
of Christianity in which this synthesis has not already been
completed. However far back we go in the history of Christianity, we never find any primitive form in which the historical Jesus, with His words and example, was all that men
had. Even in the Synoptic picture of Jesus we find the
same synthesis combining the historical Jesus and the experience of the eternal. Here also it is expressed in names
like Son of Man, Messiah, Son of David, the Son, and so
forth; for in all these names there is included the consciousness that in Jesus we have a centre of religion. How far this
goes back to Jesus Himself, or how far it is an elaboration
of the primitive Christian community, expressing its own
faith and experience, is no doubt a question of the very
greatest historical and exegetical interest. But its importance is no more than historical, and it is fundamentally

61

irrelevant to our investigation of the essence of Christianity and the permanent element in Christianity. Even if it could be historically proved that Jesus Himself did not describe Himself as Messiah—a thing which so far has not been made in the least degree credible—or that Jesus Himself did not complete this and similar syntheses, even this would be of no significance for our present purposes. We, too, have described these syntheses as religious elaborations. It is more or less irrelevant for our purposes whether Jesus Himself gave His disciples the lead in this religious elaboration, or whether He left it to themselves. It is irrelevant because we have seen that the elaboration is necessary to the essence of Christianity; and we have seen that it is only intended to give expression to what is already implicit in that essence. The hypothesis that Pauline Christology has roots which stretch back through Messianic beliefs to Judaism, and through Antiochian belief in the Kyrios back to Hellenistic influences, is a matter for exegetes and historians to judge. If it were proved that Christianity has borrowed materials from Judaism and Hellenism for its 'syntheses' and religious 'elaborations', that would not make the slightest difference to our investigations. We are already well aware that Christianity is a force that can adopt and refashion and assimilate the most diverse elements. In this, too, it demonstrates its permanent character and living power.

FIVE

Evangelical Christianity

WE HAVE indicated in main outline what is to be
accounted the permanent element in Christianity, the
element that is more or less present in all forms of Christianity, and distinguishes them from all other forms of religion. It now remains for us to notice that type of Christianity which goes by the name of Evangelical Christianity,
in order to see how far the essence and specific nature of religion and of Christianity finds expression in it. Naturally
we cannot attempt here to give an account of the content of
Evangelical Christianity, but must presume that to be
known. We shall simply examine it at certain important
points in the light of our preceding discussion. We shall
consider Evangelical Christianity from three points of view:
that of the life of the spirit, that of religion, and that of
Christianity.

(1) The place of religion in the life of the spirit is such that
all real spiritual life is ultimately founded upon it. The
source of the life of the spirit is to be found in the realm of
religion. Religion has therefore an ineradicable tendency
to insist on being omnipresent, to embrace the whole of the
life of the spirit and, indeed, the whole of life itself. There
is something irreligious about the very attempt to isolate
any sphere of life in such a way that religion has no business
there. For the religious man, there is nothing either great
or small that in itself falls outside the scope of religion.
Everything can and must be viewed in the light of eternity.
Religion is like a net spread over the whole of existence, a
net with meshes so fine that no single moment in life can

slip through it. How far does this tendency to omnipresence receive its due in Evangelical Christianity? And how does Evangelical Christianity compare with Roman Catholic Christianity in this respect?

No one can be very long in a Roman Catholic district without noticing traces of the Roman Catholic Church. New proofs of its existence and presence confront us at almost every step. The multitude of churches and religious houses; the coming and going of priests and ecclesiastical functionaries; the monk and the sister of mercy in the varied yet easily recognizable robes of their orders; the confessional, where everything in daily life is brought under the scrutiny of religion; the sanctioning and solemnizing of popular and national festivals with ecclesiastical processions and the like; the crucifix at the junction of the road; the image of the saint in its niche on a public building or private house; the effigy of the Madonna on a postage stamp; the imprimatur of ecclesiastical authority on scientific work—all these are random examples of the way in which the Roman Catholic Church intervenes in practically every department of life and allows nothing to remain outside its own province.

Evangelical Christianity appears by comparison to lead a far more modest and retiring existence. The religious question, even where people are not entirely indifferent to it, appears to be no more than one element among many in the life of the spirit, and it seems impossible to speak of its all-embracing significance. One might think that the great stream of life flowed past Evangelical Christianity completely undisturbed.

In such circumstances we cannot help asking whether the native tendency of religion to seek omnipresence does not come into its own far more in Roman Catholicism than in Evangelical Christianity? Has not the claim of religion to embrace life as a whole been understood and made real by Roman Catholic Christianity quite otherwise than by Evangelical Christianity?

At first sight it may appear to be so. But on closer examination this soon proves to be merely appearance, and in reality the position is quite the reverse. Despite the fact that Catholicism aims at a unified religious culture, it is well known that the Catholic conception divides life into two distinct and separate spheres: a lower, secular sphere, and a higher, religious and spiritual sphere. This dualism corresponds to the duality of the Catholic ideal. On the one hand there is the higher ideal, that of saints and monks, which is only realized by a few select souls who acquire a higher degree of merit by it; and on the other hand there is the lower, secular ideal of the majority, an ideal which cannot reasonably be refused recognition, although from a religious point of view it is naturally inferior. With this latter the great majority of people must be content; and they must supply the deficiencies of their life from the Church's rich treasury of the superabundant merits of the saints. Thus on the Roman Catholic view there are spheres of life which in themselves fall outside the province of religion. Everything, indeed, is of this character, which cannot be reckoned as 'religious activity' in the narrow sense of the term. But when religion and life have been dissociated in this way, the common life must then be hallowed through being brought into contact with the religious life. With this in view, the Roman Catholic Church stretches out its tentacles in every direction. It seeks to draw all alien spheres into its own province, and so to hallow what it has previously declared to be in itself profane. The Roman Catholic Church patently strives to be omnipresent, to dominate everything and to set its seal upon everything in life; but that is not because the tendency of religion to omnipresence, its tendency to allow no single moment of life to slip by it untouched, has achieved realization in Roman Catholicism. On the contrary, its efforts in this direction are an expression of the fact that religion is circumscribed within a limited sphere in Catholicism; religion is excluded in principle from other spheres of life, and it can exercise no influence upon them except by approaching them from outside, dominating them from outside, setting its seal, its imprimatur, upon them from outside.

Luther was the first to overcome this dualism and make religion again into something that embraces the whole of human life. To serve God does not mean—as Catholicism has always conceived it to mean—merely participating in directly religious exercises, or performing on certain particular occasions some special work that is well-pleasing to God. No, the whole of life is to be a service of God. That is a simple consequence of Luther's new idea of faith. He has learnt to regard faith both as the essential expression of the religious life, and also as the power by which the whole life of the Christian is carried and impelled. He can therefore no longer accept the Catholic view, which makes distinctions within that life between one department that is religious and others that are not. If faith is present in a man, then religion embraces his whole life; everything in his life is a divine service, even that which in outward aspect is most profane. If faith is absent, then religion is nowhere to be found in a man's life; even his 'religious activities' are no real divine service, for 'such things even usurers, adulterers, and all kinds of sinners can and do perform daily'.[1] In the same sermon Luther attacks the Catholic view as follows: 'If you ask them whether they hold it to be good works when they work at their trade, walk, stand, eat, drink, sleep, and do all kinds of works for the maintenance of life or for the general good, and whether they believe that God is well-pleased thereby, you will find that they answer No! and that they tie up good works so tight that they consist only of praying in church, fasting and alms-

[1] Luther, *Sermon on Good Works* (1520).

66

giving. The other works they regard as vanities which God does not inquire after. Thus they cut down and belittle by their unbelief the service that is due to God; for service of God is everything that is done, spoken, or thought in faith.' 'If a man finds in his heart the assurance that it pleases God, then it is a good work, even though it were so small a thing as picking up a straw. But if the assurance is not there, or if he has doubts about it, then the work is not good, even though it awakened all the dead, and though the man gave himself to be burned. St. Paul teaches this in Romans 14: "Whatsoever is not of faith, is sin." In this faith all works are alike, and the one is as the other; here all distinction between works disappears, be they great, small, short or long. For works are not well-pleasing to God for their own sake, but for the sake of the faith which is, works, and lives in every work without distinction, however many and various they may be.' This is the point at which Luther was able to introduce the idea of 'vocation'. He could bring the secular vocation with its manifold concerns within the purview of religion, as being in the fullest sense a divine service. Ordinary secular work is not something that separates us from God; it is a form in and through which we have to perform our service to Him, a form in which we can do this even better than in all self-chosen and more conspicuous forms of service to God.

Evangelical Christianity agrees with Luther's view, and it too puts religion at the centre of life. There is no moment in life which in itself falls outside the sphere of religion. Religion seeks to permeate everything—not by domination from without, like Catholicism, but by leavening from within. That is why Evangelical Christianity has no social or political programme of its own to offer as an alternative to other forces which seek to construct society on another pattern. It is convinced that the Christian religion will transform social life, since it is the ultimate force in the universe. But it will not do so directly by setting up a

67

Christian social and political programme which it could try, from its own higher standpoint, to impose upon society from without. Harm is always done to Christianity when it is confused with a social movement. The primary task of Christianity is purely religious—as Evangelical Christianity has fortunately never been able to forget. Its task is primarily to transform men, to fill their lives with eternal content. It is only by the roundabout way of this religious task that Christianity can succeed in working indirectly towards the transformation of social life. When it has created men filled with eternity, each one of whom serves God in his own vocation, there must inevitably be a gradual transformation and Christianization of society. Christianity has no completed programme suited to all times and circumstances. What it can do, however, is to set the circumstances, that vary so greatly from age to age, in the light of an eternity which is necessary and valid for them all alike; and it can create men who know how to solve the problems of their time with all the seriousness of eternity, men who in the very act of doing this stand in the presence of God as His servants.

In Evangelical Christianity the tendency of religion to omnipresence comes into its own in a way which from a religious point of view cannot be surpassed. We must, however, admit unreservedly that, aware as it is of its inward omnipresence, it has often missed what is necessary from a practical and pedagogical point of view in order to make the all-embracing significance of Christianity an actual reality. When the ideal is as exalted as it is in Evangelical Christianity, there is always a danger that those who are unable to aspire so high will regard it as if it did not exist at all. The omnipresence of religion can easily be turned into its opposite, so that it is not really present anywhere. When Christianity becomes a real power in a man's life, it cannot be denied that in its Evangelical form it has a significance far more comprehensive than in the Catholic form, a significance that embraces the whole of life in all its aspects. But where Christianity has not yet come to play any decisive part in a man's life, the situation is reversed. For a person who is indifferent to religion, the religious factor is, in Catholicism, an element far more often forced upon him from outside, so that he cannot wholly neglect it; and therefore it becomes, with or without his consent, one of the determinative factors in his life. It can be said with truth that the religious weakness of Catholicism has become its pedagogical strength; or alternatively, that the religious strength of Evangelical Christianity can easily become its pedagogical and practical weakness. There is little progress made in this world in the absence of a programme with certain outwardly definable concrete aims. Therefore the lack of a programme—for which Evangelical Christianity has often been blamed, and which none the less is dictated by its deeper religious conception—has often been a hindrance to it, and has prevented it from attaining the importance it could otherwise have attained by reason of its inner worth. Because it has no programme, Evangelical Christianity has been largely ignored in the treatment of individual and social problems, although it often possesses exactly what is required for their solution. From the point of view of results, more is often done by working with a not too idealistic programme than by beginning with the transformation of the human disposition. There can however be no doubt which of these two methods is superior from a religious point of view. In practical and pedagogical matters Evangelical Christians may have something to learn from other quarters; but Evangelical Christianity must not be weakened in the process, and there must be no sacrifice of depth in order to gain in breadth.

(2) A further characteristic of religion within the life of the spirit is that it is an end in itself, and does not seek the justification for its existence outside itself. In other words, religion may never be treated as a means to some other end.

69

It is an element in the life of the spirit which commands respect for its own sake, and not for its usefulness in other directions. We must therefore ask how far this second characteristic feature receives its due in Evangelical Christianity. And again we can best demonstrate our point by contrasting it with Catholicism.

It is a distinctive feature of Catholic piety that everything in it can be understood as the expression of an egoistic search for blessedness. This appears plainly at every point. What provokes the eagerness to perform as large a number of 'good works' as possible? It is not the idea that by this means increased merit is gained in the sight of God? And the greater the merit, the greater the degree of blessedness that can be claimed as reward. What is sought in the sacraments? The gifts of God's grace, which culminate in eternal blessedness. What is sought from the saints? Help to deliver men from all kinds of need. Why do monks practise asceticism in the monasteries? Luther answers in his pointed fashion: 'These things they do not in order to mortify the flesh, but they store them up as good works in order to win great merit, in order to obtain a higher place in heaven than other men; so that it might well be called a fleshly sacrifice of their bodies, which pleases not God but the devil'. Abstinence from earthly happiness is practised in order to win still greater happiness in heaven. Everything is nicely weighed and calculated. The entire Roman Catholic system is fundamentally eudemonistic. Man's happiness, man's blessedness, is central; everything in religion, even God Himself, is merely a means for the realization of this end. It is impossible therefore to say that religion is in this case an end in itself. In religion as here conceived, God is not sought for His own sake; he is sought as the one who guarantees man's blessedness. What man seeks in religion is his own happiness; that is, in the last resort he seeks himself and not God. In a word, Catholicism is not theocentric but egocentric; man and not God stands at the centre. Man and his eternal happiness is the end; God is the means to that end.

Medieval mysticism already saw that this egoistic and eudemonistic character was one of the chief weaknesses of Catholic piety; but Medieval mysticism was not successful in overcoming it, in spite of all its efforts to mortify and annihilate the self and attain complete absorption in the Deity. For the Medieval mystic, too, his experience of God takes the form of enjoyment of God; and he seeks his moments of blessedness more or less for the sake of the satisfaction which accompanies them, beside which all other enjoyment and happiness pales. Despite all tendencies to the contrary, the religion of the mystic is ultimately a religion of enjoyment; it is eudemonistic piety. This fact shows that the mystic still remains on the ground of Catholic piety.

Luther is the first to break completely with the eudemonistic piety which sees in religion merely a means for the satisfaction of man's desire for happiness. Luther is quite clear from the outset that to seek God as a means to an end is a perversion of religion. Hence he complains that even things supposed to be done in the service of God are so interwoven with the craving for enjoyment, the desire for rewards, and self-seeking. 'In all that they do they seek their own, and do nothing without calculation and to the glory of God'. Luther seeks no earthly blessings in religion; indeed he does not even seek heavenly blessings. It is not blessings that he seeks, but God Himself. That is the reason for his classic translation of Psalm 73[25]. That verse reads: 'Whom have I in heaven but thee? And when I have thee, I care for nothing upon earth.' But this is not enough for Luther. Even things heavenly pale 'when I have thee'. So he translates: 'When I have thee, I care not a whit for heaven and earth.' Here all desire for blessings is quenched. God is all in all. Beside Him there is no room to desire any further blessedness. 'For this is what it means to be blessed;

71

it is when God reigns in us and we are His kingdom.' In religion Luther seeks God for His own sake. 'Even if Christians knew that there was no heaven, no hell, nor any reward, they would none the less serve God for His own sake.' Here religion has become an end in itself in a way that cannot be surpassed.

Our next question is, how far Evangelical Christianity gives expression to the essence of religion. We shall touch very briefly upon its position in relation to the essential religious questions—the revelation of the eternal, the judgement of the eternal, reconciliation with the eternal, and eternal life. Anyone who knows Luther's experience—in which the very foundation of Evangelical Christianity is laid—will have no difficulty in discovering what part these elements played in it.

For Luther, the revelation of God was the self-evident starting-point, without which he could never have entered upon the Evangelical path. His problem was not whether a God exists, and if so, where He is to be found. His problem was rather: How shall I find a gracious God? He did not set out, like a modern inquirer, to search for an unknown God—a search in which there is often more speculative interest than religious seriousness. Nor was God for him, as for the mystic, remotely transcendent, so that a man must work his way by great effort through certain stages to God.

God was overwhelmingly near in Luther's experience; the eternal world was no mere abstract somewhat, situated beyond the bounds of this life. The Judgement of condemnation was not a dimly perceived possibility after death, but he experienced it as a present reality. This nearness of God, which is so forcefully expressed in his writings and hymns, was Luther's special privilege, and it was this that enabled him to experience the religious situation in its other aspects also with such originality and power that Evangelical Christianity still has to sit at his feet and learn of him. In his case the revelation of the eternal is concrete experience of the eternal. Whatever may have been the importance of mysticism in his religious development, his life is rooted none the less in 'revealed religion'. We have proof of this not least in the part played in his experience by the seriousness and judgement of the eternal, the consciousness of sin. His first encounter with God becomes a judgement upon his life. 'Dread is God's greeting at the first, just as when we see how the lightning shatters a tree or slays a man.'

Few men have felt the terrifying seriousness of the experience of God as Luther did. This was what made the third main question of religion so urgent for him, the question of a *modus vivendi* between the Holy and the sinner, a question we can phrase in Luther's own way: How shall I find a gracious God? It is also clear from this why Luther could never be satisfied with the answer which Catholic piety offered him, and why he was bound to attack with all his might the Catholic idea of works and merit, as an idea that merely leads men astray. The idea of possessing merit in the sight of God is self-contradictory. We can only think of such a thing so long as God is merely a name to us, merely an abstract idea. When God confronts us, as He confronted Luther, in the full concreteness of experience, in overwhelming majesty and holiness, then everything of our own dwindles into utter worthlessness. In so far as they claim validity in the sight of God, our own works become sin; they become a blasphemy against His holiness, a disparagement of His majesty. Heap high as we will our own worthlessnesses one upon another, we can never produce anything worthy in the sight of God. However many noughts we add to nought, however much we multiply nought by nought, the result is always nought. In the presence of God, only that is fitting which bears within itself His own character. The coal that can cleanse has to be taken from the altar —this experience of Isaiah became Luther's also. The atonement and reconciliation must come from the Lord. It must

73

be bestowed on us as a gift, not as the result of our works and efforts. That is why 'by grace alone' became a watchword of the Reformation. In relation to God we are never giving, but always receiving. And God requires of us nothing else but that. 'Since He is God and an almighty Lord, He willeth also to have the glory of giving us far more and more glorious things than anyone can think or comprehend; for He is like an ever-flowing spring, which, the more there wells up and flows out of it, the more it gives from its supply. He requires nothing higher of us than that we should pray for many and great things from Him; and we offend Him when we do not boldly and confidently pray and beseech Him for something. For if the richest and mightiest emperor were to offer a beggar the liberty to ask what his heart most desired, and were ready to give him imperial and great gifts, but the fool would not ask for more than a miserable dish of broth; then he would rightly be looked upon as an arrant knave, that poured scorn and derision on his imperial majesty's behest, and was not worthy to come any more into the emperor's sight. In like manner it is the greatest dishonour to God, who offers and promises us so much unutterable good, if we contemn His inexhaustible goodness or doubt whether we can obtain such things.' [2] 'He is a real God, who gives and does not take, who ministers and is not ministered unto, who teaches and governs and is not taught or governed; in a word, He does and gives everything, and has no need of anyone.' Luther never tires of insisting that receptiveness is the only right attitude to God, whereas all that savours of merit or our own works injures our relationship to God. He wishes to eradicate the last remnants of self-centredness. And these remnants are not least dangerous when concealed in the holiest of holies where atonement and reconciliation are to be effected. Luther's sound religious instinct has discovered that the zeal for works is simply another expression of the

[2] From Luther's *Larger Catechism*.

self-centred spirit, and that such zeal is therefore nothing but a sin dressed up in religious clothes. We have already seen (pp. 71–2) how he attacks the egocentric (eudemonistic) religion in which man seeks God merely in order to obtain all kinds of blessings from Him, and not for His own sake; that is, the religion in which one's own self plays the central role as master, and God becomes its servant. But Luther attacks no less emphatically the apparently opposite form of religion, in which man definitely acknowledges God as Lord, and himself as God's servant, whose duty it is to fulfil God's will by his works; for in the last resort this religion also lands us in an egocentric piety. Here, too, we come back indirectly to the self as the real centre, because the self is the giver and God the recipient. In the last resort, therefore, it is one's own self on which everything depends. Both these forms of egocentric religion must be attacked— both that in which the self is central as the recipient of God's services (Catholic eudemonism), and that in which the self is central as the giver, doing works and rendering services to God (Catholic moralism, 'work-holiness'). Both these forms of religion must be destroyed, for only then can religion become what it must essentially be—theocentric. Then, and only then, God is all in all, the centre of our life, the One who both gives and requires everything.

The answer is now plain to the fourth essential question of religion concerning fellowship with God and the indwelling of God. If God is the centre of our life, then Evangelical Christianity has succeeded in realizing the word of the New Testament: 'I live; and yet no longer I, but Christ liveth in me.' Luther's comment in his great work on the Epistle to the Galatians is extremely apt, when he writes: 'This is the ground on which our faith is sure: it takes us out of ourselves and makes us look away from ourselves to what is outside us, that is, to the promise and truth of God.' Set free from ourselves, guided and governed by the spirit of God, the Spirit of Christ—this is the aim of Evangelical

75

Christianity; this is the essence and meaning of Evangelical faith.

In giving our account of Evangelical Christianity as it appears in the context of the spiritual life and in the light of the essential religious questions, we have been continually obliged to speak of 'faith' and of 'Christ'; and these are, in fact, inseparable from Evangelical Christianity. So far we have mostly seen what distinguishes Evangelical piety negatively from Catholic piety; but here we find its positive character. Faith, the receptive attitude, is the Evangelical disposition in the strictest sense of the term. 'God and faith belong together,' says Luther. But 'in faith Christ Himself is present'. In our relationship to God we are from first to last recipients. Yet this is far from meaning that we are condemned to passivity, or to living with idly folded hands. Such is rather the behaviour of the selfish ego. In faith we receive a new centre for our life, and this must find expression. Evangelical Christianity, therefore, sets faith in indissoluble connection with love. The meaning of this fact, and indeed the whole meaning of Evangelical Christianity itself, cannot be expressed better than Luther puts it at the end of *The Freedom of a Christian Man*. He writes: 'A Christian lives not in himself, but in Christ and in his neighbour: in Christ through faith, and in his neighbour through love. Through faith he ascends above himself into God; from God he descends again beneath himself in love, and yet remains all the time in God and in His love.' God's love is received and grasped in faith; in love it is passed on to the brethren. In faith the Christian is taken out of himself, and gains a new centre for his life in God and in Christ. Then his activities, as they issue from this new centre, become the works of love.

It cannot escape anyone's notice that as far as its outward existence is concerned Evangelical Christianity is faced with a critical situation at the present time. In the midst of political upheaval, social need and strife, and personal inner distress, people sometimes look to religion and Christianity for help. When they do so, it is clear that external factors will have a considerable influence with them. Hence it is not surprising that Evangelical Christianity is often regarded as the least equipped to meet the needs of the age. We should bear in mind at this point, however, that the value of any form of religion is not determined ultimately by its political or social usefulness, but is dependent upon its purely religious value. No doubt the present situation furnishes us with abundant grounds for self-examination; but most of the criticisms of Evangelical Christianity are directed against it from a non-religious point of view. It has nothing, we are told, to compare with the close organization and the authority of the Roman Church—as if the essence of religion or of Christianity consisted of organization and authority! Or it is viewed with disfavour because it lacks a social programme to set against others that are offered—as if the essence of Christianity consisted of a social programme! As if it were merely a communal life and not eternal life! We may readily admit that Evangelical Christianity has something to learn on these points; yet it is still possible that its weakness in these respects may prove to be its strength. It has been preserved by these deficiencies from disastrous compromises, and has been able to concentrate on its purely religious task. The purely religious question was all that mattered to Luther, and just for that reason he succeeded in interpreting the essence of Christianity more clearly than anyone else. Furthermore, this religious concentration has time on its side in the long run. The need of our time is ultimately not so much programmes of reform or organizations; its need is to have eternity flung into its midst to act as a leavening and transforming power. We need Jesus Christ to come again into our life, as in past ages, bringing His

77

revelation of the Eternal, the judgement of the Eternal, atonement and reconciliation, fellowship and communion with God.

To secure this is the great task of Evangelical Christianity. If it fulfils its task, we shall be able to say of it that it 'hath chosen the good part, which shall not be taken away from it'. It, too, possesses something permanent, something of eternal worth amid the changes and chances of time.

THE ATONEMENT AS
A WORK OF GOD

Preface

THE THOUGHT of atonement, which is of fundamental importance for all real religion, is in a quite special sense the central issue for Christianity, inasmuch as the message of the Cross of Christ contains the whole of Christianity. Luther is right when he characterizes Christian theology, in distinction from all other theology, as *theologia crucis*, 'the theology of the Cross'. From this centre, from the 'word of the Cross' and of reconciliation, there radiate direct lines of connection with everything that is in any way truly Christian: the love of God, the incarnation, justification, the forgiveness of sins—all these find their focal centre in the idea of the atonement.

Throughout the history of Christianity men have wrestled with the problem of the atonement. Every age has made its contribution towards the understanding of its meaning. Much in these contributions may have to be regarded as misinterpretation, but the significant thing is that men have never been able to leave the question alone. In the brief discussion of this important and far-reaching theme, which occupies the following pages, it need hardly be said that we make no pretence of covering all its varied aspects. Our intention is rather to look at the idea of atonement from a quite definite point of view. Our treatment of the subject might well be described as 'reflections on 2 Corinthians 5^{18-19}'. Everything centres in the thought of atonement as God's own work, something done by God himself. To look at it in this light seems to be the best way of bringing certain essential aspects of the atonement into clearer view.

ONE

Atonement and Fellowship with God

THE MEANING of religion is fellowship with God. All real, living religion aims ultimately at a life together of God and man. This elementary fact must be the starting-point for our discussion of the problem of atonement.

Now this might well appear so elementary and obvious as not to need to be explicitly stated; but experience proves the contrary. For we know from experience how easily the discussion of religious questions slips unawares out of the field of religion and strays into the intellectualistic and metaphysical realm. The personal relationship with God is replaced by a religious world-view, and instead of fellow-ship with God we have an idea of God or, more vaguely, an opinion about God. We seem, of course, to be speaking all the time about one and the same thing, namely God, yet it is surely plain that the meaning is quite different. In spite of the common terminology, we are moving in the two cases within two widely separate worlds. In the first case we are dealing with a religious question, in the second with a metaphysical.

The transition from the religious to the intellectualistic, metaphysical level is doubly disastrous in the discussion of such a central religious issue as that of atonement. Here it is more than ordinarily important to be quite clear about the fundamental starting-point. For at the very outset we make a decision which affects our whole view of the ques-tion of atonement. If we start with an intellectualistic, metaphysical conception of religion, then atonement in the Christian sense will very naturally seem to be relatively superfluous. If on the other hand we have come to see that

83

the meaning of religion is fellowship with God, then atonement will be the most necessary thing of all. And why such different results must inevitably be reached from these different starting-points, it is not difficult to see.

It is characteristic of the intellectualistic, metaphysical conception of religion that it transforms religion into a religious world-view. But if we are only concerned with a religious world-view, or with metaphysical ideas about God and His nature, we can clearly occupy ourselves with them without ever seriously raising the question of atonement. We can devote ourselves to abstract speculations about the divine, or even sink ourselves in contemplation of God's holiness and righteousness, without this in any way bringing to life the need for atonement—in so far, that is, as God is conceived merely as an object of thought. There is no direct relation between God and man. Communication has been broken off, and the thought of God can therefore have no immediate, vital relevance for man.

The situation is entirely different in real religion. Here we are no longer concerned merely with metaphysical speculation. What is involved is the establishment of a relationship of communion between man and the divine. Religion claims to be fellowship with God, it claims to bring about an actual meeting between God and man. Therefore the question of atonement is inescapable for religion; it is indeed its deepest and most central question.

From a purely phenomenological standpoint also, it is plain that fellowship with God and atonement belong inseparably together. Universally, wherever a man feels that he stands in the immediate presence of God, one and the same reaction on his part is observed. The consciousness of God becomes a consciousness of judgement. To stand before God is to have judgement passed on one's whole existence, it is to feel oneself unclean and a sinner. This can be illustrated by biblical examples, such as the saying, 'Depart from me; for I am a sinful man, O Lord' (Lk 5⁸), or Isaiah's word: 'Woe is me for I am undone; because I am a man of unclean lips, and I dwell in the midst of a people of unclean lips: for mine eyes have seen the King, the Lord of Hosts' (Isa 6⁵). A man knows himself to be in the immediate presence of God; but just there he has for the first time a really clear consciousness that he cannot stand before God. The immediate relation to God creates the immediate consciousness that man, as he is, is not fit for fellowship with God.

Religion is fellowship with God. But by that very fact it faces man with the question, how God and man, the Righteous and the sinner, can be in accord with one another. Must not God in relation to sinful man be as a consuming fire? Who can see him and live?—It is here that the idea of atonement has its origin. It is not an idea resulting from free speculation, not a conception reached by theorizing, but it is born of the tension that arises in a situation where it is both necessary to stand before God and at the same time impossible to do so. 'Depart from me, O Lord!'—that is the instinctive expression of the fact that a tension exists which demands release. But the only real solution lies in atonement. For the very meaning of atonement is the creation of conditions such that God and man can meet each other.

From one point of view the whole history of religion is nothing else but a ceaseless attempt to create these conditions. At every stage of religion, therefore, and in nearly all its forms, we find all kinds of purifications, means of expiation, and atoning sacrifices. It shows little understanding of what is really involved when, as has often happened, these phenomena are regarded as a rather external affair and dismissed as merely 'cultic' observances. Such they may appear to be, if religion is thought of in an intellectualistically attenuated form. For then, of course, the religious 'ideas' are the main thing, and anything else that belongs to the phenomena of religion is regarded as a more

85

or less unessential clothing of these ideas. But in real religion, sacrifices and means of atonement are certainly not mere externalities. In them, rather, the heart of religion beats. These sacrifices and means of atonement are precisely intended to make possible fellowship between God and man.

TWO

The Three Stages of the pre-Christianity of Sacrifice

IT IS POSSIBLE to distinguish, broadly speaking, three stages in the pre-Christian and non-Christian approach to atonement and the idea of sacrifice. The relation between them may be described by saying that each successive stage includes a criticism of its predecessor.

The first stage is represented by sacrifice in its common, original meaning, whether it is conceived as a magically effective rite or as a freely offered gift. When man in the presence of God becomes conscious of his unworthiness, he seeks to cover it by means of the gifts which he offers. By offering something of what belongs to him, he seeks to appease the wrath of the deity and win for himself its favourable regard and blessing.

The second stage in the development of the idea of sacrifice is reached when man realizes that ordinary sacrifices are not adequate to reconcile him with God. 'Hath the Lord as great delight in burnt offerings and sacrifices, as in obeying the voice of the Lord? Behold, to obey is better than sacrifice' (1 Sam 15$^{22-3}$). 'To do justice and judgement is more acceptable to the Lord than sacrifice' (Prov 21^3). Here a significant new depth is found in the religious relationship. That which is to effect the reconciliation is no longer something external to man, but is the surrender of the heart in obedience to God's will. This might be called the moralistic way of reconciliation. Access to God is secured by means of ethical attainment. In no small measure this idea is dominant in the religion of the Old Testament. It is often encountered in the prophets and it finally culminates in Pharisaic piety, which by no means represents, as is often supposed, a religion of merely outward legal observance, but also in a number of ways consummates the prophetic tradition.

But there is still a third stage, and on the basis of it criticism can be levelled against this whole religious attitude. Are man's obedience, righteousness, and love really pure enough to serve as an atoning, reconciling sacrifice with which God can be well pleased? Is not such an offering rather a form of human self-exaltation over against God? Is it not a form of pride, which least of all befits a man when he draws near to the Holy One, and which therefore, so far from being a means of atonement and reconciliation, actually increases man's guilt and arouses God's displeasure? In the presence of God there is only one thing that befits a man: humility. 'The sacrifices of God are a broken spirit' (Ps 51[17]). It is when a man humbles himself and lays no claim to possess any worth, that his unworthiness is covered and the way to fellowship with God is opened for him. This way of atonement also, the way of humility, is represented in Old Testament religion. It is the fundamental thing in that type of Old Testament piety which is so strongly critical of the Pharisaic way of salvation —the piety of the 'anawim'.[1]

[1] The 'meek' of the Psalter. The word would be better translated 'humble', remembering that it describes, not an attitude to men, but a relation of humble submission to God. In reference to their social status they are called the 'poor'. (Translator's note.)

THREE

The Christian View of Atonement

WE HAVE NOW come to the very threshold of the New Testament and the Christian conception of atonement and reconciliation. How is this conception related to the idea of atonement which we have so far been discussing? The answer, if we may anticipate our conclusion from the outset, is that it is related to it as at once its fulfilment and its radical abolition.

The Cross of Christ is a plain confirmation of the fact that it is not merely the result of a human delusion when the demand for atonement is continually raised afresh among men. There is a real necessity for atonement and reconciliation between God and man. No fellowship with God without atonement, no atonement without sacrifice— this fundamental principle, which constantly recurs throughout the entire history of religion, has received here its final and complete recognition. In this sense, therefore, the Christian idea of atonement is in agreement with the pre-Christian and non-Christian idea, and is related to it as its fulfilment.

When, however, we describe the Christian conception as the fulfilment of the idea of atonement, we must not be understood to mean that it constitutes a fourth and final stage in addition to the three stages mentioned above. It can rather be said that the possibilities given there have already been exhausted. We have traced the idea of atonement and sacrifice to its extreme limit. Man offers to God something of his own; he goes farther and offers himself in works of righteousness, mercy and love; and finally he offers even the claim he might make on the basis of these,

offers it in humility. This is as far as it is possible to travel
on that road. From the external sacrifice we have moved
farther and farther in towards the centre of the religious
life. Sacrifice has developed an inwardness, a spirituality
and an intensity which cannot on this level be surpassed.
There remains nothing more to be sacrificed.

Even so, we have still not found real atonement. All
these different kinds of sacrifice have something about them
which disqualifies them as means of reconciliation. Every
attempt on man's part to put himself right with God and
make himself acceptable to God, conceals ultimately a piece
of human presumption. There is an inner contradiction in
all human attempts to make atonement and effect reconciliation. For by the very fact that he seeks reconciliation,
man acknowledges God's right to make demands on him,
acknowledges Him to be God. Yet at the same time he
denies the divinity of God, when he imagines that by means
of something of his own—his gifts, his righteousness, or his
humility—he can put himself right with God. He obli-
terates the distance between himself and God. Not least is
this true of the way of salvation by humility, even though
it apparently gives God His due. Humility as a propitiatory
act is the greatest conceivable self-contradiction. Atonement ought to mean that God and God's will are given
unqualified affirmation; but instead, what happens is that
man seeks to give affirmation to himself and his own quali-
fications in the sight of God.

Over against this the Christian view of atonement stands
for the complete abolition of the common idea of atonement. No fellowship with God without atonement—that is
true; only, atonement is not a work of man, but of God Himself. No atonement without sacrifice—this principle, too,
retains its validity in Christianity; only, it is not man who
offers the sacrifice and not God who accepts it, but it is God
who sacrifices Himself in Christ. Christianity is not the
demand for an atonement and reconcilation which man

must effect so as to open the way for himself to fellowship with God. Christianity is the *word of reconciliation*, the message of how God has made a way for Himself to us so as to bring us into fellowship with Himself. This is nowhere more clearly expressed than by Paul when he writes: 'But all things are of God, who reconciled us to himself through Christ, and gave unto us the ministry of reconciliation; to wit, that God was in Christ reconciling the world unto himself, not reckoning unto them their trespasses, and having committed unto us the word of reconciliation' (2 Cor 5[18–19]).

FOUR

Theocentric and Egocentric Atonement

THE FOREGOING discussion has shown how the Christian idea is diametrically opposed to the ordinary view of atonement and involves in the last resort its radical abolition. In order to understand the deepest reason for this contrast, we must now return to the point from which our discussion started. We affirmed there that religion is fellowship with God, fellowship between God and man. But such a relation of fellowship will have a quite different content according as its centre of gravity is located in God or in man. In the former case we speak of a *theocentric*, in the latter of an *egocentric*, fellowship with God.

As the term itself suggests, egocentric religion is hall-marked by the fact that the self and its interests take first place. Religion is here understood in terms of 'desire'. God comes into the picture essentially as the 'highest good', or that which more than all else can satisfy man's desires and needs. In theocentric religion, one the other hand, God is all in all. When man seeks fellowship with God, it is not in order to obtain blessings either of a lower or a higher kind, but quite simply because God has taken him captive and compelled him, so that he cannot do anything else but seek fellowship with God.

The contrast between egocentric and theocentric religion now presents itself in a double form. In egocentric religion the self stands at the centre (1) in so far as fellowship with God is conceived as serving man's own interests (eudemonism), and (2) in so far as fellowship with God is thought to be established by man's own actions (moralism). In theocentric religion God stands at the centre in both these

92

respects, since (1) what is sought in religion is fellowship with God for his own sake (ethically), and (2) fellowship with God is established by God's own action (evangelically).

If we desire a brief formula to express the difference between the two types of atonement and reconciliation which we have described, we might find it in connection with what has just been said, by distinguishing between a theocentric and an egocentric type of atonement.

The ordinary, non-Christian idea of reconciliation is egocentric in two respects: it starts from man himself and leads back to man himself. It starts from man himself, in that the atonement is conceived as man's own achievement, as based on something that man himself does. It also leads back to man himself, in that the ultimate effect of the atonement is to enable man to claim a standing for himself with God.

The Christian idea of atonement, however, is from beginning to end theocentric: it both starts from God and leads to the point where God and His will receive unqualified affirmation. This means, in the first place, that God is the subject in the work of atonement and reconcilation: 'God was in Christ reconciling the world to himself.' Secondly, and in consequence, the ambiguity is dispelled which otherwise always attaches to the idea of reconciliation. When man accepts the atonement that proceeds from God, he does not thereby acquire or claim any standing of his own with God, but instead he acknowledges God to be in the right.

If, however, this contrast between theocentric and egocentric atonement is used to distinguish between the Christian and non-Christian views of atonement, it should be strongly emphasized that we must beware of drawing such a distinction in too rigid and mechanical a way. Even in pre-Christian religion tendencies in a theocentric direction can be observed, and there is doubtless no religion in which no trace of theocentricity can be found. The pre-Christian theocentric tendency appears most plainly in the religion of the Old Testament. Its finest documentation is in the scene at the call of Isaiah (Isa 6$^{1-7}$). When the prophet in the presence of the glory of the Lord cries out, 'Woe is me! for I am undone; because I am a man of unclean lips, and I dwell in the midst of a people of unclean lips: for mine eyes have seen the King, the Lord of Hosts,' the narrative at once proceeds: 'Then flew one of the seraphim unto me, having a live coal in his hand, which he had taken with the tongs from off the altar: and he touched my mouth with it, and said, Lo, this hath touched thy lips; and thine iniquity is taken away and thy sin purged.' The meaning is unmistakable: it was from the altar that the coal had to be taken which could purify; it was from the Lord that the atonement must come. The theocentric tendency here is undeniable. But as has been said, these are only occasional glimpses. It is in Christianity that theocentric atonement and reconciliation first meet us clear and unconcealed. Here for the first time it can be said without any reservation: 'All things are of God, who reconciled us to himself through Christ.'

FIVE

The Compromise within Christianity

IF WE TURN to Christian theology, however, and consider its treatment of the problem of atonement, we cannot say that it has generally succeeded in following Paul and making everything proceed from God. In consequence, it has been able to give only very imperfect expression to the Christian view of atonement. The theologians have re-coiled from the idea of theocentric atonement, and where they have not simply been content with the common, ego-centric idea, they have at most sought to effect a com-promise between that and the theocentric.

A compromise of this kind appears in the assertion that it is Christ as man (qua homo) who has made the atone-ment and reconciled men with God. Admittedly, the inten-tion in this has not been to deny that atonement is a divine work. Yet the emphasis on the human element in it is not merely an incidental feature, but a symptom of the general attitude underlying this view. The starting-point here is the idea that atonement is strictly speaking man's respon-sibility. It is man that has transgressed against God; it is therefore man that should atone for the transgression, that should offer the atoning sacrifice. But since man himself was not in a position to do this, Christ as the representative of humanity has done it in his stead. What a long way this takes us from Paul! What Paul says is not, 'We were in Christ as our representative, reconciling God to ourselves or ourselves to God,' but: 'God was in Christ reconciling the world unto himself.' There is nothing here about man or humanity as the subject of reconciliation. The recon-ciliation in Christ is God's doing and nothing but God's doing; that is the fundamental thing in the Christian view of reconciliation.

It is interesting to observe the character of the general assumptions underlying a compromise of this kind between the egocentric and the theocentric ideas of atonement. They can be described in pictorial terms more or less as follows. Up there in the heavenly world, God dwells in transcendent holiness, while down here, in separation from God, man lives a life stained by sin. It is impossible for God the Holy One and man the sinner to meet, unless atonement is made and reconciliation effected. Some change or adaptation must take place. The only question is, which of the two parties is to be adapted to the other? God being immutable in His holiness, nothing can be done on that side; and indeed, according to the logic of this view, nothing ought to be done on that side. The fault does not lie in God's holiness, but in man's sin. Surely we do not expect God's holiness to make overtures to sin and adapt itself to that? The necessary change must come to pass on man's side. Man must be changed and brought into conformity with the holy will of God. Sin must be brought to an end, or if that is more than man can do, it must be neutralized by an appropriate atonement. In short, man must be conformed to God's holiness. When that has been done, and only then, can there be any thought of fellowship with man on God's part. God's holiness has then secured what it is bound to require, and the way lies open for fellowship with God on the basis of holiness.

Now obvious and natural as this way of thinking may seem to be, it is none the less a direct contradiction of the Christian view of atonement. It is like a slap in the face for everything that is at all central for Christianity. No matter which of the basic presuppositions of Christianity we select—the incarnation, the life and work of Jesus, or His death—at every point the contrast between the Christian faith and the view just described is only too evident.

For what else is the Christian doctrine of incarnation but an affirmation that God Himself has come to us here in this world of sin, and that His holiness has not prevented Him from entering into fellowship with sinners? And what else is the whole life of Jesus but a proclamation that the Holy One seeks to have dealings with sinners? It is significant that when Jesus speaks of the purpose of His mission, He interprets it by saying: 'I came not to call the righteous, but sinners' (Mk 2[17]). Again, if we turn finally to the death of Christ, this also bears witness, as Paul interprets it, to exactly the same thing: for 'while we were yet sinners, Christ died for us.' Moreover, Paul immediately goes on to apply this to reconciliation, saying: 'While we were enemies, we were reconciled to God through the death of his Son' (Rom 5[8,10]).

What does this mean for our present purpose? It means that in Christianity there can be no thought of atonement and reconciliation as something accomplished by man. *The atonement is from first to last a work of God.* This statement must be given full weight, and must also be applied without qualification to the atoning work of Christ. Any attempt to replace the Pauline 'God was in Christ' with 'Christ as man (qua homo)' means that something of the common, egocentric conception of atonement is smuggled into the Christian view.

With this we have reached the point that is ultimately decisive for the Christian view of atonement. There remains, however, one difficulty still to be solved. For even when it is admitted that atonement in the Christian sense is not a human work but wholly divine, the question can still be asked whether there is not after all some truth in the thought of Christ as our representative, the representative of humanity. What makes this question so serious is its apparent connection with the idea of the vicarious significance of Christ's sacrifice. Is not the vicariousness of Christ's sacrifice and suffering an aspect of His atoning work with which Christianity cannot afford to dispense? And if that is so, does not the alternative proposed above— either a divine or a human work—lose its meaning? For if Christ's suffering is vicarious suffering, whose 'vicar' or representative is He if not ours? Does it not therefore follow that Christ's atoning work, divine though we may claim it to be, involves in the last analysis a reparation or satisfaction made to God in our name and on our behalf? In other words, *Christus qua homo!*

In this argument, ideas which are acceptable from a Christian point of view are closely interwoven with others which are not. The idea of vicarious suffering, for instance, undoubtedly stands for something quite central to the Christian view of atonement, and something that can never be given up—a point to which we shall return in another connection later. But if we seek to conclude from this that the atoning work of Christ means a satisfaction made to God from our side and on our behalf, we put ourselves at once outside the characteristically Christian conception of atonement. It is, of course, not difficult to understand the motives that underlie this continually recurring idea of a satisfaction made to God on our behalf. It is entirely natural that a man who seeks to return to God should feel the need to make amends for what he has done wrong. The idea of reparation or satisfaction, however, is commonly criticized on the ground that it presupposes an impersonal, legalistic and external conception of sin and the expiation of sin; that it involves man in an unspiritual bargaining with God, as if the main thing were the paying of damages, regardless of who pays them, whether the guilty party or someone else in his place; and that it therefore lacks insight into the personal and ethical character of sin and the way in which sin can be overcome. Now this criticism may apply to the vulgar forms of the idea of satisfaction, but it has failed to grasp the deepest intention of that idea, which is precisely of a personal and ethical nature. It is as if the work of atonement and reconciliation could not be regarded as adequately carried out except in terms of a satisfaction rendered to God, and as if it could not on any other understanding lead to complete and unclouded communion with God. If it cannot be said that everything of which man has robbed God by his sin has been compensated to the last farthing, then it looks as if there must be something lacking in the atonement. It is as if there were still some obstacle in the way of full fellowship with God, and as if this obstacle could only be removed from man's side. For even if God in His goodness were willing completely to disregard man's sin, and to receive him into fellowship in spite of it, the relationship between God and man would still not be entirely in order. If man for his part is to be able to accept this fellowship, then even though no one else demands it, he must demand of himself that he do what is right and make amends for his transgression. And it seems to be in virtue of the ethical consciousness itself that he must make this demand on himself. The motive behind the idea of satisfaction can thus be in the deepest sense ethical. At least, this idea may be dictated by the concern that the atonement shall be entire and complete, leaving no trace of sin behind to be felt, inevitably, as a disturbing factor in the religious relationship.

Nevertheless, from a Christian point of view this line of argument must be set down as totally misleading. The desire we so naturally feel in our human relationships to meet our obligations and not be in debt to anybody, becomes in relation to God nothing less than an attack on His divinity. If a man says, 'I cannot accept fellowship with God unless I myself first fully meet all my obligations,' that is simply an attempt cloaked in ethical terms to gain standing for himself with God. It means that he puts himself on a level with God, or refuses to acknowledge God as God, by refusing to accept anything as of grace. In this sense there cannot and ought not to be any satisfaction made. We can never stand before God as anything but debtors. Fellowship with God is always something that exists 'in spite of sin'. The interpretation of the atonement in terms of the formula 'all is paid', which has often been used in Christian preaching, can of course be rightly understood as an expression of the absolute validity of the atonement. What it means then is that there is nothing which any longer stands in the way of man's fellowship with God. Yet this formula is not without risk. It can easily be taken as an expression of the unchristian thought that since 'all is paid' God has got what is His due, and we now have a right to fellowship with Him and to a share in His blessedness. The same righteousness of God which, so long as sin was unatoned, prevented Him from receiving us into fellowship with Himself, must now—since 'all is paid'—require Him to accept us as His own. It is easy to see that such a conception is nothing but a caricature of the Christian understanding of atonement. But one is driven in this direction as soon as any place at all is given to the egocentric tendency in the theocentric scheme of atonement.

Fellowship with God on the Basis of Holiness or of Sin?

IF WE MAY venture a paradoxical expression of the contrast between Christianity and the usual idea of atonement, it can be stated as follows: Fellowship with God on the basis of holiness—that has been the age-long dream of humanity; fellowship with God on the basis of sin—that is the new message of Christianity, for it is exactly what 'the word of reconciliation' implies. Or, to put the same thing in less paradoxical terms: atonement does not mean that we from our side, either of ourselves or through representatives, raise ourselves up out of our human, sinful life to the divine realm, and so enter into relations with God, meeting Him as it were on His own level; but atonement means rather that God lowers Himself to us and associates with us on our level, in spite of our sin.

We are here at the point where the difference between Christian and non-Christian views of atonement shows itself more plainly than anywhere else. Yet, oddly enough, there is hardly any point at which more confusion exists both in theology and preaching. Even when the Christian idea of atonement is recognized as in principle theocentric, so that reconciliation is exclusively a divine work, the revolutionary consequences of this for the whole religious situation are as a rule far from being realized. It is in order to bring out these consequences in full relief that we have propounded the possibly offensive and certainly paradoxical thesis that Christian fellowship with God is a fellowship on the basis of sin.

We shall now proceed to develop this thesis in rather

more detail, dividing it for convenience into the two following propositions: (1) It is not holiness that leads to fellowship with God, but fellowship with God that leads to
holiness; and (2) Fellowship with God has not man's holiness as its aim, but is an end in itself.

(1) *It is not man's holiness that leads to fellowship with
God, but fellowship with God that leads to holiness.*

To man's natural way of thinking it seems self-evident that
God will have dealings only with one who is holy and
righteous, and that the sinner is debarred by reason of his
sin. The way to fellowship with God, therefore, appears to
be that of the successive overcoming of sin. When sin is
removed, and only then, is man fit for fellowship with God.

Now it is by no means necessary to go outside Christendom to find this conception represented. We can find it in
Roman Catholicism. The difference between Catholicism
and Evangelical Christianity is commonly described by
saying that the former directs man to self-salvation in the
strict sense of the term, while the latter points him to the
grace of God. There is undoubtedly sound observation
behind this description. Yet we fail to do full justice to the
Catholic position, if we describe the Catholic way of salvation quite simply as self-salvation. For the Catholic Church
has known ever since Augustine, that man left to himself
would be lost, and that he can do the good only with the
help of divine grace. The decisive difference does not lie
precisely where it is commonly supposed to lie, but at a
still deeper level. It has to do with the religious relationship
itself. In Catholicism it is a question of fellowship with
God on the basis of holiness, whereas in Evangelical Christianity it is a question of fellowship with God on the basis
of sin. In other words, the Catholic view remains essentially on the level of natural thinking, and the specifically
Christian conception of fellowship with God is not given
full weight till the Reformation.

The contrast here in question between Catholic and

Evangelical Christianity finds remarkably clear expression in their different ways of speaking about justification. When it is said that God 'justifies' man, this is only another way of saying that he takes man into fellowship with himself. The controversy over the doctrine of justification, therefore, is not—as it is often taken to be—simply a dispute about an isolated point in dogmatic theology and its theoretical formulation, but it concerns the structure of the religious relationship itself. When it comes to showing on what terms man is received into fellowship with God, the ways of Catholic and Evangelical Christianity part.

The Catholic way finds expression in the watchword 'faith formed by love' (*fides caritate formata*). Over against this Luther sets his watchword 'faith alone' (*sola fides*). Now it is true that Catholicism, too, can speak of 'justification by faith', but it always has to add that this is not a matter of 'faith alone', but of faith in so far as it is perfected by love, or (in the Aristotelian terminology usually employed) 'formed' by love. 'Form' is the valuable thing, which imparts value to 'matter' by impressing its stamp upon it. Catholicism now applies this idea to the relation between faith and love, *fides* and *caritas*. Faith is 'matter' (*materia*), and as such insubstantial and powerless. Love is the 'form', the formative principle, which by means of setting its stamp upon, or 'forming', faith, gives it value and true being. It is thus ultimately not by faith but by love that man is justified and comes into fellowship with God.

What is the reason for this extraordinary interest in love, which Catholicism displays? The answer is not far to seek. Love is the fulfilling of the law. The whole requirement of the law is comprised in the commandment of love for God and one's neighbour. If this love is found in a man, then all righteousness is thereby fulfilled. He is no longer a sinner, but holy. So if, in accordance with the formula '*fides caritate formata*', God justifies a man and takes him into fellowship with Himself because of the love (*caritas*) which he finds in him, then the old idea that it is only with the holy and righteous that God has dealings, remains completely intact. 'Fides caritate formata' thus becomes the classical expression for fellowship with God on the basis of holiness. With the sinner God has no fellowship. God can enter into relations with a sinful man only if and when He has remodelled him, so to speak, and made him something other than he was. On this view, therefore, the way to fellowship with God proceeds through two stages: first, God has to convert the sinner and make him holy by an 'infusion of love' (infusio caritatis); then he can take this remodelled and sanctified man into fellowship with Himself.

Against this whole idea Luther raises his protest. He more than anyone else has understood the saying of Jesus, 'I came not to call the righteous, but sinners', and the assertion of Paul that it is precisely the sinner whom God justifies. He more than anyone else has understood that God's love is a will to fellowship which does not allow even our sin to set limits to it, but in utter self-sacrifice stoops down to us and wills to have dealings with us in spite of our sin. To this loving will of God, this divine will to fellowship, faith holds fast. Man cannot, it is true, base his justification, i.e. his acceptance with God, on any love existing in himself and making him holy and righteous in God's sight. On the contrary, as far as his own condition is concerned, man is always in God's sight a sinner. But this does not mean that he is excluded from fellowship with God. It means that his fellowship with God rests on a quite different basis, namely on the fact that it is precisely with sinners that God in Christ seeks fellowship. That is why Luther can speak of the believer in Christ as simul justus et peccator, 'both righteous and a sinner'. Hence sola fides becomes the classical expression for fellowship with God on the basis of sin. In this way the theocentric conception of atonement and reconciliation at last gains full acceptance.

The same thing is expressed in other terms when Luther
opposes the Catholic view that a man must do good works
in order to merit salvation and blessedness, with his well-
known assertion that a man must be blessed and saved
before he can do good works. In order to see what he really
means by this, we must first get rid of a very common mis-
understanding. It is often said that Catholicism and Luther
maintain directly opposite positions regarding the relation
between morality and blessedness, ethical and eudemonistic
value, the doing of good and the gaining of happiness.
Catholicism says: 'Do the good and you will be happy, live
a holy and self-denying life and you will gain eternal bliss.'
Ethical behaviour is thus for Catholicism the pre-supposi-
tion of happiness and blessedness. Here, however, Luther
steps in—so the argument proceeds—and completely re-
verses the situation. He sees that it is impossible to achieve
any real happiness and blessedness on these lines. Catholicism has failed to understand 'the psychology of happiness'.
It has not understood that happiness and blessedness cannot be made the object of searching and striving. Seek
happiness and you may be sure that it will fly from you.
This is even more true with regard to the deepest of all
happiness which personal beings can enjoy, the happiness
that can be described as blessedness. Blessedness belongs
at a depth in human life which is not accessible to the
influence of our works. Blessedness cannot be gained by
means of what man himself does, it is a gift of God.
Luther's importance, therefore, on this view, lies in his
insight into the psychology of happiness. He does not deny
that there is a connection between goodness and happiness,
but he does not take the common view of it which is re-
flected in the Catholic idea that happiness or blessedness is
to be earned by doing good. On the contrary, happiness
comes first, and goodness follows. Only one who is happy
can really do the good. But whether one is inwardly happy
or unhappy, does not depend on oneself. Happiness is not

something a man gets for himself, but something given to him; it is divine 'grace'.

In recent times this view has been asserted by Max Scheler, who feels obliged to agree with Luther against Catholicism on this point, and who quotes with approval—in the sense explained above—Luther's saying that a man must be happy before he can do the good. Since Scheler's religious views are otherwise based on Catholic principles, it is hardly surprising that his approval of Luther has often been noted with great satisfaction in Evangelical circles, as if he had put his finger on something that was a matter of Luther's vital concern. It must, however, be said that this involves a very crude and superficial understanding of Luther's position. As if Luther's contribution to religion consisted in the discovery of something as trivial as the psychological principle which can be expressed in the phrase 'glad and good'! As if 'grace' were synonymous, in Luther's understanding of it, with a naturally happy disposition whch looks on the bright side of life and knows how to make the best of any situation!

What is the real meaning of Luther's contention that a man must be blessed before he can do the good? First of all, we must observe that 'blessedness' for Luther does not mean an intensified and deepened feeling of happiness. Blessedness is the same as fellowship with God. A man is blessed if he lives his life in fellowship with God, even if it is a life marked, as far as feeling is concerned, with great unhappiness. Moreover, when Luther speaks of 'grace', this has nothing to do with a man's natural disposition. Grace means rather the active intervention of God's love. To speak of grace in any other sense is to misuse the word.

Now with all this it may look as if we have wandered a long way from our real subject, the Christian idea of atonement. In fact, however, we have all the time been keeping as close to it as possible. The Christian idea of atonement is unique, as we have seen, in maintaining that there can be a fellowship with God on the basis of sin. If only we now accept the fact that blessedness is for Luther the same as fellowship with God, we shall at once realize that his famous dictum about the need for a man to be blessed before he can do the good is simply a way of expressing the idea of fellowship with God on the basis of sin. It is here that the deepest opposition between Luther and Catholicism lies. Catholicism says: 'You must do good works in order to become blessed. Only the righteous are taken into fellowship with God, only the holy are permitted to "see God" and "enjoy God".' In other words, Catholicism teaches fellowship with God on the basis of holiness. In opposition to this, Luther insists that it is necessary to be blessed in order to be able to do good; that is to say, only the man who already lives in fellowship with God can do what is good. Luther has realized that fellowship with God does not rest on the foundation of holiness, but on the contrary, holiness rests on the foundation of fellowship with God. But in that case, on what basis is fellowship with God established? The answer is: On the basis of sin, or (as we can equally well say) on the basis of grace. Both statements mean ultimately the same thing, the difference between them depending simply on whether the question is looked at from man's side or God's. In the former case we say 'On the basis of sin', for as we contemplate man we find no holiness in him that could furnish a motive for God's acceptance of him; it is, in actual fact, sinners that God takes into fellowship with Himself. If, on the other hand, we look at the matter from God's side, we must say 'On the basis of grace'; for God's acceptance of man has its ground in God's 'unmotivated' love, which, in order to emphasize its 'unmotivated' character (in the sense that it is not 'motivated' or evoked by anything in us), we usually call 'grace'.

This, then, is what atonement in the Christian and Evangelical sense means: it means that God in His grace or unmotivated love stoops down to sinful man and seeks fellowship with him. Man the sinner breaks fellowship with God. God the Holy One restores fellowship with lost man; and He restores it, not when a man has first worked his way up again to the level of God's holiness, but precisely at the point where it was broken, in the midst of man's sin. That is what Paul means when he says 'God was reconciling the world to himself' or—putting it even more clearly—'while we were enemies we were reconciled to God' (Rom 5[10]).

When Paul speaks in this way about reconciliation, he is speaking out of his own experience. He had sought fellowship with God on the basis of holiness—but found it on the basis of sin. During his time as a Pharisee he had sought fellowship with God on the foundation of holiness, by observing the law and practising righteousness; but by that means he had only succeeded in getting as far away from God as possible, having become a persecutor of the Church of God. But what attitude did God take to this sin of his? Just when he was in the midst of it, God opened the way for him to fellowship with God. It was this experience that made Paul outstandingly a preacher of grace.

Now there is a widespread idea that fellowship between God and the world must presuppose that the power of evil is first broken. Otherwise, it is thought, reconciliation would simply mean that God reconciled himself to evil and abdicated his holiness. And it is of course a matter of supreme importance that nothing should be allowed to obscure the opposition between God and evil. This fact, however, must not lead us to limit or weaken the assertion that what Christianity offers us is fellowship with God on the basis of sin. That assertion remains true without qualification even here. The position is not that the dominion of evil must first be broken in order to make fellowship with God possible; it is rather that the dominion of evil can only be broken by man's living in fellowship with God.

We have looked in some detail at the proposition that it is not holiness that leads to fellowship with God, but fellowship with God that leads to holiness. To this we must now add the second and no less important proposition that:

(2) *Fellowship with God has not man's holiness as its aim, but is an end in itself.*

The reason why Christian fellowship with God is a fellowship on the basis of sin, is that God is love and his love is 'unmotivated'; which means that it is beyond all rational calculation. To reason it seems self-evident that God seeks fellowship only with the righteous. Christianity preaches the opposite: God seeks fellowship with the sinner. This strikes all our ordinary thinking as so unprecedented, that even when we recognize it as being the unique thing about Christian fellowship with God, we would still like to find some way of rationalizing it and making it more acceptable. It then often happens that the statement we made above, about fellowship with God leading to the conquest of evil, is used for the purpose of such a rationalization. We start with the conviction that God has appointed holiness as the goal for man, and that he really ought not to take anyone into fellowship with himself except one who is holy. If, however, it is certain that holiness can be attained only on the foundation and with the help of fellowship with God, then God's acceptance of the sinner into fellowship is simply a sign of the wisdom of his dealings with men. It is the only way in which he can make the sinner righteous and holy. The idea that God wills to have fellowship with sinners, absurd and offensive as it is in itself, ceases to be offensive and becomes thoroughly understandable as soon as we realize that, far from God's holiness being surrendered, its purposes are served, since the ultimate aim is man's sanctification.

From a Christian point of view, however, rationalization of this kind must be rejected on two counts.

To begin with, it is based on an egocentric conception of religion which is incompatible with Christianity. How is it that the idea of fellowship with God as a means of attaining a holy and perfect life finds such ready acceptance? The answer is not far to seek. We feel it is beyond question that the perfecting of one's own life is an end in itself, having a value of its own, which needs no further motivation. Everything else has its value determined by the extent to which it promotes this ultimate aim. Hence if it can be shown that human life reaches its fullest perfection only through man's fellowship with God, then the relevance of fellowship with God is established. This is one of the basic ideas with which apologetics has always worked; but it is an idea with an egocentric bias. Why should I believe in God and seek fellowship with God? Because only so can I find full satisfaction for my deepest needs, only so can the latent possibilities within me be fully realized—that is the answer of traditional apologetics. As if it were not sufficient for us simply to be received into fellowship by God! As if we needed to justify our wanting anything to do with God by the good and advantageous results which follow from it in our lives! No! it is of the essence of Christian fellowship with God, that it can never be sought as a means to some other end. If we have our eye on something else beyond God, however excellent it may be, then it is no longer God that we seek. To find a motivation for fellowship with God in something else is the same as a denial of fellowship with God. From a Christian point of view, nothing can be more senseless than the attempt to justify fellowship with God by reference to its significance for the things we ourselves value most; for in the presence of God all the things that we value are radically called in question. In Christianity it is God who is absolutely certain, while the values of our life are problematical; what sense is there, then, in seeking to base the former on the latter?

In the second place, the view that makes holiness the aim

of fellowship with God, is open to the objection that it involves a denial of divine love in the Christian sense, a denial of God's Agape. When Christianity speaks of God's love for sinners, this is explained as meaning that what God really loves is not so much the sinner as what can be made of the sinner. It is not the sinner as he actually exists in his present concrete situation, that God loves, but the sinner in so far as he still has within him an uncorrupted kernel of goodness with which divine grace can make contact so as to turn him into a holy and perfect man. When God seeks fellowship with sinners, it is not because he really desires fellowship with them, but because that is the only chance he has of transforming them into righteous men with whom he really can desire fellowship. In a similar way, the idea of justification also is reinterpreted. When God justifies the sinner, he sees him, not as the sinful man he actually is, but as the saint he will one day become. That is to say, God's justifying of the sinner means that He anticipates his future perfection.

Now it is undeniable that by this means we can considerably reduce the offensiveness of the idea of God's love for sinners, of which Christianity speaks. But the price paid for this is far too high; for it involves the surrender of what is most characteristic of the Christian idea of love, so that we are no longer able to speak of God's love as spontaneous and unmotivated. In that case there would be no real will to fellowship, and therefore no real love, behind the fellowship with God. How very different from the divine love revealed in Christ! When Jesus says, 'I came to call sinners', a call to repentance and amendment is certainly included. But this does not mean that love is the means and amendment the end. Love is always an end in itself, and the moment it is degraded into a means to some other end it ceases to be love. Fellowship with God has its meaning entirely in itself; and just as it is a perversion of fellowship with God when a man seeks it in order to gain something else (even his own ethical perfection) by it, so it is a perversion also when behind God's will to fellowship we look for something else that might furnish a motivation for it. On God's side, too, the fellowship is an end in itself.

Perhaps the idea that fellowship with God must not be regarded as a means to some other end, may seem to be merely a theoretical abstraction without any practical significance. It is a fact that God in his love wills to recreate man. Why then can it not be said that God's love is the means and man's holiness the end? Nevertheless, it is of the utmost practical importance that divine love should not be thus treated as a means to an end. An example may make this plain. The objection is sometimes brought against Christian charitable activity—not always without justification—that it is used far too much for the purpose of religious propaganda. When men cannot be won by direct methods for Christianity, they may perhaps be won indirectly by being treated as objects of Christian love. Even to an outsider there is something insulting about this use of love for an ulterior purpose, excellent though the purpose may be. The love is not then real and genuine. It is of course true that a Christian who loves his neighbour longs to win the neighbour for Christ. But this does not mean that love shown to one's neighbour in his physical need must be a means to that end. Its meaning lies wholly in itself. Christian love helps simply and solely in order to help. We find it offensive when human love does not give itself freely and without any ulterior motives; how then can we maintain that divine love is a means to some other end? No! God is love; and when He loves, he has no further end in view. Fellowship with God, on God's side also, is an end in itself. To live in fellowship with God certainly means for man to be recreated in the image of God; man's sanctification is the fruit of his fellowship with God. But the fellowship does not therefore cease to be an end in itself, nor does God's love cease to be spontaneous and unmotivated.

SEVEN

Atonement and God's Agape

W E HAVE NOW reached a point where atonement and divine love can be seen to be simply different ways of saying the same thing. When we are told with regard to reconciliation that 'all things are of God', this means that reconciliation or atonement has its sole source in God's love. But the relation between God's love and atonement is in fact even closer than at first appears from this statement. They are not two separate things, but essentially one and the same. We cannot speak of either without at the same time speaking of the other. God's love is in its essential nature Agape-love; it is downward-moving love, a love which seeks the lost and wills to have fellowship with sinners, a love which is spontaneous and creative of fellowship. But nowhere does its creative character find clearer expression than when it encounters man's sin. Sin breaks fellowship with God, God's love restores it; it is reconciling and forgiving love. It is in full harmony with this, that Christianity has always found the supreme manifestation of divine love in the atoning death of Christ. Thus Paul says: 'God commendeth his own Agape toward us, in that, while we were yet sinners, Christ died for us' (Rom 5⁸); and in the First Epistle of John we read: 'Hereby know we love, because he laid down his life for us' (1 Jn 3¹⁶). To speak of God's love and leave atonement out of account is to rob love of its divine depth. On the other hand, to speak of atonement and not to mean by it exclusively a work of divine love, is no longer to speak of atonement in the Christian sense of the word.

This unbreakable connection, this identity between

E.C.—8   113

God's love and atonement, is of the utmost importance when we are dealing with the Christian idea of atonement. For in it we possess the criterion by which every theory of atonement can be tested with regard to its Christian content. Any theory of atonement which conflicts with the love of God, with God's Agape, is from a Christian point of view to be condemned. All that we have to say in what follows, has no other purpose than to make clear this connection and identity between atonement and the love of God. Just because of this identity, however, a fresh difficulty arises, which we must consider a little more closely. If atonement and God's love are one and the same, why talk any longer about atonement? Is it not enough to speak quite simply of God's love?

Does not God's Love
make Atonement superfluous?

IN WHAT has been said so far, we have shown how the theocentric view which Christianity takes of the relation between God and man, involves a radical abolition of the usual idea of atonement. It completely excludes the idea that we, by offering some sacrifice of our own, could reconcile ourselves with God. The work of reconciliation is all on God's side. 'All things are of God.' But this raises a question of a very serious kind, which requires fuller discussion.

For it might well be asked whether the abolition of the usual idea of atonement has not been made so radical, that not only the egocentric conception of atonement, but all atonement whatsoever has been abolished? If literally everything is of God, in the unqualified sense described above, why should we any longer speak of atonement at all? Is not the thought of atonement the relic of a belief which Christianity has rendered obsolete, and do we not by retaining it simply confuse the whole issue and prevent ourselves from seeing how truly everything is of God—that is, how everything is grounded solely in God's love, which is eternal and unchangeable and therefore needs no atonement? Cannot the position be stated simply and directly as follows: God is love, and just because He is love He can, when He is faced with man's sin, do nothing else but forgive it? Is it not therefore enough to speak of God's love and forgiveness without bringing in anything about atonement? Do we not obscure and belittle God's love if we speak of atonement in this connection, as if that love would not give itself directly and without any intervening atonement, and as if it were not entirely self-evident that God, who is love, forgives sin?

Support for this view has been found in the Bible, and particularly in the parable of the Prodigal Son. In this parable it has been argued—Jesus depicts God as the Father, who in his love welcomes the repentant son when he returns home, and welcomes him without any reservation. Jesus inserts no reference to his own atoning death as the ground of forgiveness. The only ground of forgiveness is God's own love and mercy. Later Christian belief about atonement has therefore no connection with Jesus's own thought, but is rather in irreconcilable conflict with it. The gospel Jesus proclaims is simply the message of self-evident forgiveness. Everyone finds it quite natural that an earthly father should overlook his son's errors and forgive him, since in spite of all errors he is still his own son; and just so Jesus would teach us in this parable to see it as self-evident that God, the heavenly Father, forgives us our sin if only we are heartily sorry for it. The view represented here can be briefly summed up in the statement that since God is love, all talk of atonement is superfluous.

In fact, however, it is hardly possible to conceive of any idea which, from a Christian point of view, is more fundamentally wrong than this. It is open to objection in many particulars, and not least with regard to the misinterpretation of the parable of the Prodigal Son and the arbitrary use that is made of it. But we must confine ourselves here to dealing simply with the main contention, with regard to which we must insist that the actual situation is the exact opposite of what is here maintained. According to this view, God's love is supposed to make atonement superfluous; but in point of actual fact it is precisely God's love that makes atonement necessary. If God were not love, then conceivably there might be no need for atonement.

NINE

Atonement as the Synthesis of God's Holiness and God's Love

THE ATONEMENT is often represented as the synthesis of God's holiness and His love. The fact of sin, it is argued, has not simply altered man's situation, but has also had an effect upon God. As a result of sin there has arisen a tension between God's holiness and His love. Because of His holiness God must condemn sin, but in his love He wills to forgive it. His holiness stands as an inescapable 'must' in the way of His purposes of love, making it impossible for Him to realize them without first satisfying the demands of holiness. What this tension means can be expressed negatively as follows: because of his love God cannot condemn, because of his holiness he cannot freely forgive. Atonement, however, furnishes the means of releasing this tension. In the atonement love triumphs over holiness, but in such a way that holiness also gets its due. In the atonement love has found a way to forgive which holiness can accept. God's holiness demands atonement and God's love provides it.

This is undoubtedly a much profounder view than the one last described, and as a reaction against the superficial idea of self-evident forgiveness it has been of considerable importance. Yet with regard to the real state of affairs, it too must be said to be misleading. The error of the previous view is not overcome by adding holiness to love as a corrective of love's will to forgive freely, and so making atonement necessary. We are still working with what, from a Christian point of view, is an inferior conception of God's love and forgiveness, as if these were the same as sentimental love and easy indulgence. What is more, even the proposed corrective fails of its purpose; for even a just judge can in certain circumstances, without any surrender of the principles of justice, dispense with punishment. Such a dispensation, which need by no means be dictated by love, but by nothing more than simple reasonableness or equity, can often coexist with the highest justice. It is thus an inferior notion of righteousness and holiness that is used in the attempt to make up for the defects in an inferior idea of love.

As a result of dissatisfaction with this situation, some would maintain that divine love does not need to be buttressed in this way by righteousness and holiness. God's love is already in itself holy, and as such must necessarily demand atonement. It is not anything external to God's love, but its own holy character, that makes atonement necessary. But even if the superficial notion of God's love as easy indulgence is in this way excluded, the thought of 'holy love' is not without its dangers. It is all too short a step from this to the idea that it is not really the love itself, but the holiness included in the love, that makes atonement necessary. If we are to discover the true inwardness of the Christian idea of atonement, we cannot stop till we have found the direct connection between divine love and atonement. Even the last-mentioned view is open to the objection stated above, that it is precisely God's love that makes atonement necessary. The meaning of that statement can now be more precisely defined. Atonement is necessary, not because God's love is holy, but because it is love.[1] It is

[1] It need hardly be pointed out that there is here no question of setting love in opposition to holiness. On the contrary, our argument is directed against any attempt to make two different things of holiness and love. Where they have been allowed to fall apart, and divine love has begun to be spoken of in an unspiritual, sentimental sense, there may well be felt a need, on second thoughts, of adding holiness as a corrective. But the situation is in no way improved by this. We must reckon with love in its Christian depth from the start, and we must see how it is just this love that makes atonement necessary, and that atonement is basically nothing else but the entry of this love into the world of sin.

essential that we should be clear about this, because if we are not, we shall never be able to see how the atoning work of Christ, so far from implying any limitation of God's love, actually gives it its Christian depth.

TEN

God's Love makes Atonement necessary

WE HAVE SEEN above how difficult it can be, and commonly is, to combine atonement with God's love. Either we start with God's love as an established fact, and then find all thought of atonement superfluous; or else we start with atonement as an established fact, but imagine we then have to make room for it by postulating along with God's love something else which explains the need for it, such as God's holiness or certain eternal and immutable laws which prevent God's love from having free course without the intervention of atonement. However opposed to one another these two conceptions may seem to be, they nevertheless have this in common, that neither is able to bring atonement and God's love into real, inner connection with one another. The reason is in both cases the same, namely that the meaning both of God's love and man's sin is superficially understood. God's love is conceived as if it were nothing more than sentimental love, and man's sin is interpreted moralistically, as if it were simply a matter of particular moral defects and errors. By this double superficiality the fact is concealed that it is just God's love and man's sin that are the irreconcilable opposites.

As far as God's love is concerned, it is no doubt true that the sinner awakens God's inner compassion. But it is quite disastrous if this fact is used to explain away or blurr the absolute contradiction between God and sin, that is, between divine love and sin. Anyone who imagines that God's holiness stands in irreconcilable opposition to man's sin, but that God's love could more easily come to terms with it, simply does not know what God's love is.

Nor do we show that we know what sin is, if we use soft phrases about poor unhappy sinners. There may, of course, be some measure of truth even in those terms, but they refer to sin only as it appears on a rather superficial, moralistic level. They make it look as if at heart the sinner wanted nothing more than to live in fellowship with God, but that certain moral faults lie as an obstacle between him and God. Forgiveness is accordingly conceived to mean that God overlooks these defects and mistakes, and does not let them constitute any hindrance to fellowship with himself. But this is not a true picture of sin. Sin is fundamentally rebellion against God. Sin means that man, who was created by God for fellowship with God and his fellowmen, has turned away from God, thrust Him out of His place and usurped it for himself. Sin is in its essence selfishness. This is a truth often expressed, but its meaning is less often truly grasped. When people speak of sin, they generally understand it in a moralistic sense, with reference to particular moral misdemeanours, or else in the very general and abstract sense of a universal sinfulness, which is little else but another name for human finitude and imperfection. But in neither of these ways do we arrive at the Christian conception of sin. For the Christian faith it is an established fact that 'God is love', and that it is God's will that love shall rule the world. But if we take a realistic view of human life, we cannot help seeing that what prevails there is not love but the very opposite of love. Self-assertion, not love, is the universal law. Men stand as individuals or groups ranged against one another. Everything is directed, not towards giving in love, but towards getting in selfishness.

Into this world that is closed against Him, indifferent to Him, God wills to bring His love. Here above all it becomes clear that it is precisely God's *love* that makes it impossible for forgiveness to be the superficial, easy-going and self-evident thing commonly called by that name, and that forgiveness can only exist in inseparable connection with a real atonement. The sin that has to be forgiven is not simply a matter of a few moral misdemeanours standing in the way of God's loving purposes; therefore forgiveness cannot simply mean that God magnanimously overlooks these faults and pursues His purpose of love without regard to them. The sin consists precisely in the fact that man selfishly shuts himself up against God's love, showing no interest in it, and in so far as he seeks God at all, he seeks Him for selfish ends, so that—as Luther puts it—'even in God he seeks only his own'.

Now what—in this situation—can forgiveness mean? Is it not a word simply without any meaning? When sin is given a moralistic interpretation, it is certainly not difficult to understand what forgiveness means. It means simply that God overlooks man's transgressions of His commandments, and grants him His fellowship in spite of them. But when sin means that man is unwilling for fellowship with God, what sense is there in talking of forgiveness? Can it mean that God overlooks even this sin, so that He does not even ask whether man is willing to accept His love or not? It would surely be a strange kind of love that desired to give of its riches to the one whom it loved, and yet did not care whether he accepted or rejected them? Love is a will to fellowship. If it were indifferent to the response of the loved one—his willingness or unwillingness to enter into fellowship—then it would no longer be love. Love cannot, without ceasing to be love, fail to demand a real at-one-ment. The breach which makes fellowship impossible must be filled up. And how else can this be done than by selfish humanity ceasing to be selfish and laying itself open to divine love? This seems to be the only possibility. Selfishness must be sacrificed in order that love may prevail.

If that happened, fellowship with God would be possible on the basis of holiness. But that is not what happens. Selfishness is by no means prepared to submit to love without more ado, and to renounce and sacrifice itself. It is thoroughly unrealistic to talk about the power of love as if the mere existence of love were enough to make sin and selfishness give way. Instead, love must take upon itself the burden which selfishness has caused but refuses to bear. In this way love becomes what Luther calls *eine verlorene Liebe*, lost love, in the strictest sense of the term.

ELEVEN

Lost Love

HERE WE approach the deepest mystery of the atonement. God's love and the selfish world: these are the two great opposites. Every attempt to describe the contrast in other terms weakens it. We do not heighten, but diminish it, if we substitute God's holiness for His love; and we diminish it also if we interpret sin, not as a selfish perversion of the will, but moralistically as particular acts of transgression. Once we realize, however, that the opposition is between just these two, God's love and man's selfishness, we can immediately see what a gulf yawns between them. It is never self-evident that they can be brought together. Here something must be sacrificed. Selfishness sacrifices nothing, least of all itself. God, the divine love, takes the sacrifice upon Himself instead. 'God was in Christ reconciling the world to himself.' Here in the most literal sense it is possible to speak of vicarious sacrifice and vicarious suffering. When selfish human life refuses to conform to the divine love, God's love does not refuse to submit to the conditions of selfish human life. The question may be raised whether such a procedure is worthy of the divine love, and from an ordinary human point of view the answer must be that it is not. But such is divine love, such is God's Agape, that it does not allow even human selfishness to set a limit to its giving and self-giving. It comes down into the world of sin and does not hesitate to give itself away to selfishness. It becomes a sacrifice in a new and deeper sense than that in which the lover always sacrifices himself for his beloved. It suffers itself to become lost love, a love spurned and trampled underfoot by selfishness. That is the way of divine atonement. 'All things are of God, who reconciled us to himself through Christ', says Paul, and he adds forthwith the profound saying: 'Him who knew no sin, he made to be sin on our behalf; that we might become the righteousness of God in him.' We must let this saying stand in all the sharpness of its paradox. A complete understanding of what it means that Christ was made sin for us by God, may well not be possible. But this at least is clear, that it refers to something there is in common between ourselves and Christ in respect of sin. It is a matter of fellowship with God on the basis of sin, though with righteousness as the fruit of fellowship with God.

We must, however, speak with more reserve than is customary regarding the fruit of the love that so recklessly gives itself away. Reference is often made, far too lightly and with little regard for reality, to the omnipotence of suffering love, as if it were a self-evident and indisputable fact. In a well-known Swedish hymn by Geijer, the line occurs: 'Naught there is that is not gained by love that suffers.' Such a doctrine of the omnipotence of suffering love, suggestive of a semi-naturalistic metaphysic, obscures the reality of the risks taken by love. It is as if nothing of love could be wasted. But in that case the sacrifice made by love is no real sacrifice. Again and again the saying of Jesus, 'whosoever shall lose his life for my sake, the same shall save it' (Lk 9^{24}), is misinterpreted in this kind of way, as if it were merely a prudential rule for the man who wants to be sure of winning out in the end. Whereas the world only reckons with outward resources of power, Jesus is supposed to have discovered another and surer way to success, the way of love, of self-denial, of sacrifice. Even if one who takes this way seems outwardly to lose, yet he can be sure in the deepest sense of gaining by it. But what is to be said of a 'sacrifice' so motivated? It is in fact the very opposite of sacrifice. It is simply a refined form of self-assertion, all the more subtle because disguised as self-sacrifice and love.

125

But Jesus is speaking of really losing, really sacrificing, and that is possible only for a love that is prepared to become lost love.

Now it is just this that is characteristic of the divine love which meets us in Christ; it is quite really and in all seriousness a lost love. Infinitely much of the love poured out by God upon selfish humanity is hopelessly lost. When the word of reconciliation is sown, some falls by the wayside—and is lost; some falls on stony ground—and is lost; some falls among thorns—and that, too, is lost and bears no fruit. Here we have the greatest sacrifice and the profoundest suffering of love, when it becomes lost love. But God's love does not come to an end, God does not cease loving, because his love is spurned and trampled on by human selfishness, so that it becomes quite literally outcast and lost.

But where does divine love meet us as lost love more truly than in the Cross of Christ? Yet the love which does not cease to be love even when it is lost, is for that very reason the victory over all that stands against it. Here, and only here, is there any room for talk of the omnipotence of love. The way between God and a world fast bound in selfishness has been opened. Therefore the Christian faith sees in the atoning work of Christ the unshakable foundation of our fellowship with God.

TWELVE

Summary

OUR WHOLE argument may be briefly summed up as
follows:

1. The meaning of religion is fellowship with God.
Therefore the question of atonement is fundamental for
religion.

2, 3. In relation to pre-Christian and non-Christian ideas
of atonement, which appear on three main levels, ((i) sacri-
ficial gift, (ii) the way of ethical achievement, (iii) the way of
humility), the Christian conception is at once their fulfilment and their radical abolition.

4. The usual idea of atonement is egocentric, the Christian idea theocentric. The classical expression of the latter
is in 2 Corinthians 5[18-19]: 'All things are of God. . . . For
God was in Christ reconciling the world to himself.' God
is the subject in the work of atonement.

5. Christian theology has not always succeeded in following Paul. In general it has tended to be satisfied with a
compromise between egocentric and theocentric atonement. The best example of this is *Christus qua homo*,
'Christ as man'.

6. Mankind has always dreamed of fellowship with God
on the basis of holiness. Christianity proclaims fellowship
with God on the basis of sin. This is the meaning of (i) the
gospel of Jesus: 'I came not to call the righteous, but
sinners'; (ii) Paul's doctrine of justification: it is the sinner
whom God justifies; (iii) Luther's renewal of Christianity:
simul justus et peccator, 'both righteous and a sinner'.

7. Atonement and God's Agape are at bottom one and
the same. A view of atonement that does not rest entirely

on God's love, is from a Christian point of view false. God's Agape is the standard by which the Christian content of any idea of atonement can be tested.

8, 9. When the commonly accepted views of atonement are tested by this standard, we discover how difficult men generally find it to combine the thought of atonement with that of God's love. Either they start with God's love, and then find atonement quite superfluous (the Parable of the Prodigal Son); or else they start with atonement, but then are able to reconcile it with God's love only by introducing the idea of his holiness. Atonement is then conceived as the synthesis of God's holiness and His love, not as a direct expression of His love.

10. It is characteristic of the Christian view of atonement that what makes atonement necessary is precisely God's love. Love is the will to fellowship. Sin consists essentially in the fact that man does not want fellowship with God. Atonement consists in the fact that the divine love itself takes upon itself the burden which selfishness has caused but refuses to bear.

11. The atoning work of Christ is therefore in the most literal sense vicarious sacrifice and vicarious suffering. Here the divine love meets us as 'lost love'. But only the love that sacrifices itself to the point of becoming lost love, a love trampled on by selfishness, is at the same time omnipotent love. Since Christ's love on the Cross became lost love, His Cross has become a *crux triumphans*.